Answers to Questions
Nobody Was Askin'

Answers to Questions Nobody Was Askin'

And Other Revelations

Tim Sample

Down East Books

Camden, Maine

Published by Down East Books
A wholly owned subsidiary of The Rowman & Littlefield Publishing Group, Inc.
4501 Forbes Boulevard, Suite 200, Lanham, Maryland 20706
www.rowman.com

Unit A, Whitacre Mews, 26-34 Stannery Street, London SE11 4AB

Distributed by National Book Network
Copyright © 2015 by Tim Sample

British Library Cataloguing in Publication Information Available

Library of Congress Cataloging-in-Publication Data

Sample, Tim, 1951-
Answers to questions nobody was askin' and other revelations / Tim Sample.
pages cm
ISBN 978-1-60893-368-6 (cloth : alk. paper) -- ISBN 978-1-60893-369-3 (electronic)
1. Maine--Social life and customs--Humor. 2. American wit and humor--Maine. I. Title.
PN6231.M18S36 2015
818'.602--dc23
2014037504

∞™ The paper used in this publication meets the minimum requirements of American National Standard for Information Sciences Permanence of Paper for Printed Library Materials, ANSI/NISO Z39.48-1992.

Printed in the United States of America

For Joe Gelarden,
who just wouldn't take no for an answer.

Contents

VII: Zen and the Art of Storytelling

Introduction

I've known Tim Sample for more than half my life.

At the age of seventy-six, that's saying something. When you know someone that long, it's hard for them to keep surprising you—particularly because, as well as becoming accustomed to their face, you've become familiar with their style. Well, I suppose Michelangelo had a style, too, but they didn't call him a Renaissance man for nothing. And if you think that it's a stretch to compare that renowned figure of world history with Maine's own Tim Sample, well you might soon want to rethink.

Singer, artist, comedian that Tim is, this book was created much like a Swiss-army knife for your spirit. For just as helpful as the many handy blades on that imported multi-faceted tool might be, there's a chapter here for every critical moment in your life—and a couple extra for making sure you've got some future comfort stored up as well. Certainly, if you've ever heard him in concert, you may already have an inkling.

Funny, insightful, expressive—full of exaggeration and Maine lore. Riotously excessive and reverential of all things Maine, particularly the people. While the technologies of the modern world might tend to unravel those ties that bind, the stories contained in this collection tend to knit us back together again.

It might be helpful for you to know that much of my perspective comes from being born in the radio age, before television and during a time when information being delivered by spoken word over airwaves was still relatively new. The voices of Edward R. Murrow and Arthur Godfrey (to name just a few) told of events and adventures far different than anything happening in my neighborhood. But through their commentary, I believe many of us became citizens of a larger experience.

It wasn't that their stories were necessarily exotic or provocative, but more that they were authentic and revealing of a deeper and connective truth. And, as part of this community of awareness, we were encouraged to become more tolerant and respectful of other people's traditions and mindsets. It was exhilarating to realize that as unique as we each might be, there seemed to be an underlying set of ethics threading its way through all cultures and springing from some mysterious source—perhaps identifiable but not nameable.

And so, in much the same way, through these tales related by Tim, you'll come to recognize people we all know (or would delight to know) in moments that we've lived (or wish we could live). This is a must-have book. Witty enough you'll want it close at hand for reference and renewal. Profound enough you'll want it in the bathroom.

Noel Paul Stookey
Blue Hill, Maine

Only in Maine

What Mainers Don't Say

My phone rang one fine spring morning and it was Captain Kip Files on the line. Captain Files is co-owner of the Victory Chimes, which I and many others consider the crown jewel of the Maine windjammer fleet. If you feel like arguing that point be my guest. But, the next time you run across a "Maine Quarter" in your pocket change, flip old George over and take a peek. Ayuh, that's the Victory Chimes sailing past Pemaquid light. I rest my case.

Kip was pitching an idea that he and the other windjammer captains had hatched the previous winter. Each summer the fleet gathers in Penobscot Bay for the "Great Schooner Race." That year, on the night before the race, they'd all be anchored in the Fox Island Thoroughfare between Vinalhaven and North Haven Islands. They figured a Maine Humor show on North Haven would give their guests a fun activity and me an enthusiastic paying audience. "Don't talk past the close, Cappy!" sez I, "I'm onboard."

A few calls later I discovered that the school auditorium I'd hoped to use was closed for renovations. My friend Barney, a local schoolteacher and year-round North Haven islander, suggested that I call the town office about renting the new community hall. When I reached the town clerk, she sounded like she had better things to do than jaw with some humorist. As a result, her responses tended to be short but not particularly sweet and when I inquired about the seating capacity of the building the line went momentarily dead. "You still there?" I asked, "Ayuh." "Well, I need to get the seating capacity of the building so I'll know how many tickets to print." Her exasperated sigh was followed by the hollow thunk of her phone hitting the desk. I waited patiently. She eventually returned; "The seating capacity of that building is 347!" Fortunately that was my final question, allowing her to refocus on more pressing issues.

So the hall was booked, 347 tickets were printed and distributed and by the time the week of the performance rolled around the windjammer captains had sold about 300 of 'em, a solid crowd with a few tickets still available for walk ins. Sweet. The day of the show I hopped a puddle jumper from Owls Head Airport. Barney met me at the island "landing strip," a.k.a "freshly-mown field." We packed my gear into his truck and headed for the community hall.

Upon arrival we discovered two stacks of folding chairs plus two expandable bleachers. When we'd finished setting up all the chairs we only counted 118. Hmm, maybe those bleachers hold more than we'd thought. Nope. Once they were set up it was pretty clear that even in the unlikely event that all the passengers were 90-pound fashion models we'd still only be able to accommodate another hundred or so. That left over a hundred ticketed customers without seats. As I pondered our predicament I noticed a small metal sign bolted to the side of the building: "Maximum Seating Capacity 347." That's when it hit me. When I'd asked the clerk about seating capacity she had simply walked across the driveway, read the plaque on the side of the building and passed the information along to me. Seating capacity? 347! I'd asked. She'd answered. No need to toss in any extraneous details like the fact that there were only about 200 actual seats in the building!

Fortunately, Maine islanders are nothing if not resourceful. We spent the rest of the afternoon scouring North Haven for every available chair, managing to round up enough to provide seats for 320 audience members. The rest, mostly younger folks, sat on foam tumbling mats in front of the stage.

In the end everybody had a good time and I learned an important lesson, one I should have known all along. When dealing with taciturn Mainers it's not so much what they say that you need to pay attention to, it's what they leave out. I should have known it because only a few years earlier I'd released an album on which I told the one about the traveling salesman who, upon seeing an old geezer and a dog on the porch of a Maine country store, asks, "Does your dog bite!" "Nope," the geezer replies, "my dog don't bite." Thus reassured, the salesmen starts up the steps only to be viciously attacked by the dog. Once safely back in his car he rolls down the window and hollers, "I thought you said your dog don't bite?" "Mine don't," replies the geezer. "But that one right there sure does!"

The Laughter of Clams

I recently overheard a conversation in the grocery store checkout line that went something like this: "So, she told me she was 'happy as a clam' and I asked her, 'What's so happy about clams anyway?'" That's a darned good question, which deserves a darned good answer. Fortunately, as a result of having spent a half century or so exploring, collecting, examining, and recording folk tales, humorous anecdotes, similes, metaphors, and such, I've acquired a sizeable collection of these quirky one liners, including the one about happy clams. Hmmm, let's see, it's right here somewhere. Hold on a minute.

Well, I'm sure I'll find it in a moment. Meanwhile, the fact that I even have such a library of verbal ephemera at all surely stems from my lifetime membership in the Think in Pictures Club. TIP Club members, being visual thinkers, always find a good simile particularly satisfying. Perhaps that's because it allows us to remember things by connecting a verbal description to a strongly visual mental image.

In most instances, of course, I've long since lost track of where or when I originally encountered each of these conversational visual aids. But, I'm occasionally able to recall precisely my first encounter with a really memorable line. Here's an example.

My eighth grade teacher, the late, great, Melanie Stein, was one of those gifted educators capable of changing a student's life for the better—a mentor long before mentors became hip and trendy. She possessed a deep and abiding love of language as well as a real appreciation of the power of words to paint pictures. It was she who first introduced me to the notion of a group of old men on the porch of a Maine country store "sitting around with one arm as long as the other." The image of entrenched indolence, which that phrase conjures up, could not be replicated by 10,000 words.

I've also gleaned a number of gems from writers like early twentieth century Maine author, poet and humorist Holman F. Day. Day, a kind of Down East Robert Service, penned such classic poems as "Aunt Shaw's Pet Jug" and "The Tale of the Kennebec Mariner," the latter of which included the terrific simile, "dark as a cellar shelf." If you've ever spent any time mucking about "down sullah" on a quest for the last remaining Ball canning jar of Grandpa's dandelion wine, you know the particular inky blackness of which he speaks.

There's also another whole family of potent similes, which seem to spring directly from New England's deep Puritan roots. If you're casting about for an apt and memorable description of a broiling hot summer afternoon, "hotter than the hinges of hell" would certainly fill the bill. At the other end of the conversational thermometer, our moralistic forebears might have described a frigid January night that's "colder than a hussy's heart." A bit judgmental, to be sure. But the point is not lost.

An agitated Mainer is likely to be observed "jumping around like fat on a griddle," or the slightly more nonsensical, ". . . like a cat on a griddle." Fat on a griddle? Sure thing. But, a cat? You have to wonder whether the hapless feline leapt onto the stove in order to escape the notorious "hot tin roof" we've heard so much about. If so, wouldn't that be akin to jumping "out of the frying pan into the fire"? Hmmm, perhaps we'd best be moving along now.

Here's a mystery. Why is it that Mainers have singled out the poor innocent hake for such derision and ridicule? I'm referring of course to the venerable Maine phrase, "numb as a hake," used by generations of natives to describe a person who is a bit slow on the uptake. I ask you, is a hake really any more "numb" than a haddock, cod, or a flounder? I mean, they all got caught didn't they?

In case you're keeping track, no, I haven't forgotten my promise to provide an answer to the original question, i.e., "Why is the Maine clam so darned happy?" All you'll really need to solve that mystery is knowledge of the complete original phrase, which went (drum roll please) like this: "Happy as a clam in the mud *at high tide*." Those last three words make a big difference, huh? When you hear the whole phrase the meaning immediately becomes obvious. At high tide the clam diggers have no access to the clam flats! This extremely safe and secure state of affairs no doubt left our defenseless little mollusk friends "grinning like a dog eating bumble bees."

Going to the Basement

I occasionally present workshops on storytelling and the oral tradition, in which we explore, among other topics, the role of dialect and colloquialism in the traditional tales of New England. These quirky, regionally specific, often comical words, phrases, and pronunciations of everyday speech play an important role in establishing the basic ground rules of social interaction.

I suppose there will always be people who insist that the famous "Maine accent" is disappearing. Clearly they haven't been talking, or more to the point, *listening,* to the right people! Spend an hour poking around the working waterfront on the Maine coast, a hardware store in Harrington, or a sports shop in Greenville and you'll hear accents as thick as Aunt Edna's clam chowder.

It's worth noting that dialect exists universally, in all cultures and societies for exactly one purpose. A person's accent allows attentive listeners to determine, almost instantly, whether the speaker is "local" or "from away." That's important information, whether the issue is survival of the fittest or simply deciding how much to ask for that stinky old lobster trap in your yard sale.

Colloquialisms serve much the same purpose. I thought about that recently when I ran across a quirky but familiar term in a Stephen King novel. In the book, Steve uses the word "hosey." As a native Mainer I know exactly what hosey means. In my youth when somebody on the playground shouted, "I hosey the next turn on the swing," everyone knew that meant he or she was next in line. My wife, having grown up in Minnesota, knew all about a similar term, "dibs," but never heard "hosey."

There are, of course, many words and phrases that sound completely normal to locals yet are virtually a foreign language to "outsiders." Enough of them, in fact, that my former Boothbay Region High School sophomore English teacher, the late Gerald E. Lewis, wrote a bestselling book, *How to Talk Yankee,* on the subject.

Here is a short list of some of my own favorite Maine colloquialisms. You might try them on your out-of-state visitors this summer just for fun.

Cunnin': Cute, as in, "That baby of Charlotte's is some cunnin'. Lucky she don't take after her mother."

Daow: No (the opposite of ayuh). Very widely used when I was young. "You goin' to Burt's wedding next Sat'day?" "Doaw! I went to the last three and besides there's a good ballgame on."

Scrid: Small portion. "You want another plate of beans?" "Nope. Got to save room for just a scrid of Mary's rooobub pie!" For some reason in Maine and a few other spots around the country, it's always pronounced "roobub" rather than "rhubarb."

I'll finish up with a truly wacky example that I've only heard used by a handful of people in and around the Boothbay region. I'm pleased to say that this is one colloquialism for which I can personally provide what Paul Harvey used to call "the rest of the story."

A certain generation of Boothbay Harbor locals (you know who you are) attended high school or even grade school in a tall barnlike structure that once stood about halfway down School Street. One feature of the building's architecture was that some, but not all, of its bathrooms were located in the basement. Since there are at least 1001 euphemisms for a bathroom I won't attempt to list them here.

What I can say with certainty is that several generations of local folks who once attended classes in that particular school building grew up referring to the "bathroom" as "the basement," as in, " Mrs. Proctor, may I please be excused to go to the basement?"

So, if you ever find yourself in the company of a local adult of "a certain age" when they excuse themselves from the table while simultaneously mumbling something about needing to "go to the basement," you'll know that they haven't been struck with a sudden urge to check the fuse box or do a bit of impromptu oil burner repair.

Nope, they're simply making a "pit stop," taking a trip the "head," "the john," "the loo," etc. Don't let it throw you off. That's just the way we say it around here.

Roadside Attractions

I recently spent a week visiting my daughter in Albuquerque, a town guaranteed to strike fear into the hearts of spelling bee contestants everywhere. My choice of lodging during my stay in New Mexico was, as usual, based on the three Ps—practicality, price, and proximity. Many years on the road have taught me to avoid the more "interesting" and "colorful" local options. I tend to agree with the copywriters of a popular 1960s ad campaign, "The best surprise is no surprise at all."

Yet, I *was* pleasantly surprised on my first morning in Albuquerque, when I ventured forth in search of coffee, only to discover that I was just a few short blocks from old Route 66. Yes, *that* Route 66, the very tarmac upon which "Buz" and "Tod" drove their Corvette Roadster every week in the TV show of the same name, the fabled "mother road" itself! A few more blocks and a few half-remembered verses of Nat "King" Cole's finger snapping ditty later, I was ensconced in a bright red vinyl booth at the historic Frontier Restaurant, ordering from a menu listing huevos rancheros and green chile stew, among other local favorites.

While awaiting the arrival of my carne adovada and eggs, I examined the restaurant's distinctive décor, an eclectic mix of local artwork featuring lots of elaborately framed paintings and prints, uniformly rendered in the subtle earth toned palate of the southwestern desert. Providing a visual counterpoint were several XXL amateur portraits of John Wayne.

Feeling oddly comforted by the unabashedly kitschy backdrop, I found myself reflecting on America's deep and abiding love affair with "roadside attractions."

Naturally, any classic roadside attraction should reflect the unique culture of its region, and I'll admit to having spent far more time than most locating, exploring, and reporting on my own region's offerings. Of course, it helps if your "day job" involves occasionally sharing the TV screen with such legendary examples of the genre as Ken Brown's venerable, yellow-slicker-clad, pipe smoking, giant Maine fisherman.

Just like the colorful concrete and fiberglass gunslingers, teepees, and dinosaurs along old Rte. 66, the giant fiberglass fisherman, who has been keeping a watchful eye over the Brown's Wharf parking lot since I was a kid, is a larger-than-life caricature of the way we see ourselves and how we want others to see us.

It should come as no surprise, then, that some of our most memorable roadside attractions are modeled after the two characters (three, if you count the moose) featured prominently on the Maine state seal: the Maine fisherman and the Maine lumberjack.

Some of you may recall the rugged (although somewhat exhausted looking) 22-foot-tall "Maine Sardine Man," who once stood stoically in fair weather or foul, holding a giant sardine can, as the official greeter at Maine's New Hampshire border. In case you're wondering where he went, I recently caught up with him, still standing tall, clutching that same can of sardines, in the coastal Hancock County town of Gouldsboro.

Located a couple hours north of Gouldsboro and towering head and shoulders over Maine Sardine Man, Bangor's 31-foot-tall Paul Bunyan statue cuts an impressive figure (and just about anything else he wants to) with the massive double bladed ax slung across his right shoulder. If you're curious about that strange object he's holding in his left hand, chances are you're "from away." Any true Mainer should recognize that item as a "peavey," the classic logging implement designed by a blacksmith in Stillwater, Maine, in 1858, and still locally manufactured and sold over a century and a half later.

Naturally, popular roadside attractions, like Bangor's Paul Bunyan statue, tend to generate a certain amount of local pride, and rivalries have been known to develop as a result. I experienced this first hand one summer when my wife and I were visiting friends in her home state of Minnesota. Since Minnesota also has several Paul Bunyan themed roadside attractions, a debate soon arose regarding which state was the famous logger's original "home." Although good points were made on both sides, I had an ace in the hole.

Remember that blacksmith in Stillwater, Maine, back in 1858? Well, just four years earlier, two enterprising loggers from that same Maine town headed west and founded the town of Stillwater, Minnesota. Ayuh, Minnesota's first town was founded by two loggers from Stillwater, Maine!

Now, I'm not saying I can prove that either of those fellows was old Paul himself. But I figure they were at least passing acquaintances, and when it comes to roadside attractions, being a "passing acquaintance" is pretty much the whole point.

Moxie Mystery

One hot summer day when we were kids, my older brother offered me a sip from a bottle of soda he was drinking. "It's something new," he said. "You'll like it." The bottle, with its cheery orange label, certainly looked harmless enough. How bad could it be?

If you've ever unwittingly taken a big gulp of Moxie you already know the answer. The word "disgusting" leaps to mind, along with a few others, including "bitter" and that old standby, "medicinal." Had he re-filled an empty pop bottle with diluted cough syrup? Was this a practical joke? I wouldn't have been surprised if a bunch of kids had leapt from behind a nearby bush, pointing and laughing hysterically.

My brother just shrugged and took another long pull, flashing an enigmatic smile I've come to recognize as a common expression among aficionados of this particular product: a subtle, self-satisfied quasi-smirk that conveys the unspoken message, "You, my friend, are unable to appreciate the finer things in life." Thus was I introduced to Moxie, the unique beverage that, since May 10, 2005, has been canonized as Maine's official soft drink.

Moxie historians report that sometime in the mid-1870s, one Dr. Augustin Thompson, a native of Union, Maine, working in Lowell, Massachusetts, created the formula for a new patent medicine. Christening his elixir "Moxie Nerve Food," the good doctor insisted it would provide quick, effective relief from a long list of maladies, including insomnia, irritability, paralysis, and "softening of the brain." Frankly, I can't help wondering whether that last ailment may actually have been what inspired some folks to purchase Moxie in the first place.

A few years later, carbonated water was added to the recipe, and Moxie the soft drink was born. The precise origins of its unusual name remain murky. Some maintain that it's derived from a language once spoken by one of Maine's indigenous tribes. Others trace its roots to an actual *root* found only in some remote corner of a tropical rain forest.

Whatever its etymology, the word soon entered American vernacular and "moxie" is now listed in dictionaries as a synonym for "force of character, determination, or nerve." Celebrity endorsements from sports figures like Ted Williams and "Babe" Ruth sparked a sales boom and Moxie became a nationwide hit. That's right. Believe it or not, for a time in the early twentieth century Moxie was the best selling soft drink in America!

At the very least that's a testament to the power of advertising, but what about the product itself? Have you ever actually tasted it? Fortunately my job at CBS News gave me a chance to explore what has always been a baffling mystery—the true source of Moxie's continuing popularity.

And what better place to start exploring than the annual Moxie Days celebration in Lisbon Falls? This lively summer gathering attracts hardcore Moxie fans from around the globe. One year a septuagenarian Moxie-phile from Scotland won the prize for the longest distance traveled to attend the event.

Moxie Days features countless examples of Moxie memorabilia, including one of the original Moxie cars. These clever mobile billboards sported a realistic life-size artificial horse bolted to an automobile chassis. Sitting astride this horse, the driver maneuvered the vehicle by means of a massive steering wheel sprouting from the animal's neck. Examine a Moxie car up close and you'll no doubt wonder whether the designer was spiking his Moxie with something just a wee bit stronger during the critical development phase.

Quirky memorabilia aside but still no closer to unraveling the secret of Moxie's popularity, I appealed to The Moxie Man himself, Mr. Frank Annescetti. Standing behind the counter of his Moxie Store in Lisbon Falls, surrounded by Moxie memorabilia, Frank finally gave me the plausible solution I'd been seeking.

"You see," he explained, "when you take your first sip of Moxie it doesn't taste very good." I'm with you so far Frank. "But," he continued, "you take another sip and it still tastes kind of bitter. After your first bottle you aren't sure you like it. But, you try another bottle, then another. . ."

As I'm listening to The Moxie Man, light dawns and the truth hits me like a tsunami of bitter cola. Of course! A Moxie drinker never does actually *like* the taste of Moxie. That's not even the point! The point is to *endure it*!

Which also explains why the word moxie, meaning "force of character, determination, nerve," continues to resonate so deeply with Mainers. Glancing at Frank's "Moxie Makes Mainer's Mighty" T-shirt I finally realize why that slogan is true. A person has to be mighty tough just to drink the stuff!

Back to Bean's

Like a lot of my fellow Mainers, I'm a fan of Freeport's famous outdoor retailer L.L. Bean. When I was a kid, trips from Boothbay Harbor to Portland meant driving along Coastal Route 1, which runs right through the middle of downtown Freeport.

Those familiar with today's upscale mecca of outlet stores anchored by the sprawling L.L. Bean complex, would be hard pressed to imagine the town as it was in, say, 1956. Back then Freeport's "downtown" was a three-way intersection with a flashing yellow traffic light and a Flying A gas station where the attendant would gladly pump your gas and check the oil. There was a restaurant, too, as well as a Five and Ten (cent) store and, of course, L.L. Bean.

For such a popular tourist destination, the original Bean store occupied a remarkably modest three-story wood-frame structure. The store's appeal to outdoorsy types may well have been enhanced by the fact that shopping at Bean's literally required a bit of hiking. Through rain, sleet, wind, and snow, access to the upper floors was gained only via a wooden staircase on the *outside* of the building!

Although much has changed at L.L. Bean, one thing that hasn't is the company's famous customer satisfaction guarantee. The inventory system may be computerized these days. But, the basic promise remains much the same as it was when old L.L. himself was in charge: If you're not absolutely satisfied, for any reason at all, they'll replace the item or refund your money. Period. No excuses. No time limit.

I came by my appreciation of Bean's return policy the old-fashioned way: by personally schlepping stuff back to the store. Not a lot of stuff you understand. Maybe an item every decade or so and even then only when there was a genuine problem. Having been raised with traditional Yankee values, the notion of returning something for a refund, whatever the reason, holds little appeal to me. It's a bit too close to whining or to use that most onerous of Maine epithets, being "spleeny."

On the other hand, old L.L. had his values too. And back then his personality defined the company to such an extent that I got the impression he'd have been disappointed if I had a problem and *didn't* bring it his attention. So, taking him at his word, when an old pair of "Bean boots" sprung a leak I simply brought 'em back to the store and drove home with a new pair, no questions asked.

That said, the following incident (for lack of a better name let's call it The Yellow Rain Slicker Debacle) involving a canary yellow raincoat I'd purchased at Bean's several years earlier might, had it occurred on his watch, have been enough to convince L.L. to rethink his generous return policy.

A well-made, practical garment, my yellow rain slicker had given me many years of exemplary service. So, I decided to treat it to a thorough cleaning. A quick review of the garment care label instructions (obviously composed by someone for whom English was neither a first nor even a distant third language) informed me that "dry cleaning may be helpful." It should be noted that in strictly grammatical terms the instructions at least implied that dry cleaning possibly may not be helpful, an interpretation that, in this case, turned out to be right on the money.

Responding to an urgent phone call from my dry cleaner, I raced over and made the alarming discovery that my favorite slicker had been magically transformed into a huge, saffron-hued sheet of . . . what? Fried won ton? Actually, it resembled nothing so much as a gag prop from a 1970s Carol Burnett TV special.

Though I'd have much preferred to lob the thing directly into the nearest toxic waste dump, I felt a moral obligation to return it to Bean's if only to spare future generations of yellow rain slicker label readers a similar fate. The sales staff did an admirable job of keeping their faces on straight as I proceeded to manhandle the freakishly flattened, outsized yellow slicker through the showroom en route to the exchange counter.

Upon arrival, true to their word (and in record time I might add) the L.L. Bean folks replaced my favorite rain slicker with a similar model free of charge.

I'm happy to report that nearly twenty years later I still have that exact same rain slicker, although, these days it's more of a muddy mustard color. That'll happen when you wear the same yellow slicker for two decades without ever once taking it to the dry cleaner.

The Pilot Cracker Incident

When I answered my phone early one morning back in 1996, I was surprised to hear that it was my friend June Elderkin calling from Southport Island. More surprising still was her abrupt, almost accusatory, tone: "Timmy," she barked, without so much as a how-de-do. "What are you going to do about those Pilot Crackers!?" I would have been tempted to take her question as a joke had it not been for the obvious agitation in her voice.

"Pilot Crackers?" I asked, desperately seeking some conversational traction, "What's wrong with Pilot Crackers?" "There's nothin' *wrong* with 'em," she huffed. "But, they're trying to take 'em away and you have to do something about it." Eventually she calmed down enough to explain the situation and a fascinating tale began to emerge.

It was a gripping saga, which did, in fact, involve the beloved Crown Pilot Cracker, the traditionalist's first choice to complement a steaming hot bowl of Maine chowder. Also featured in the story were lots of seriously ticked off Maine islanders as well as (in the coveted role of "The Evil Corporation") the multinational food giant Nabisco.

Apparently, when Nabisco decided to stop manufacturing several of its less popular brands, including the iconic but, alas, slow selling Pilot Cracker, the corporate bean counters had no idea that, for tradition conscious Maine chowder lovers, their decision came dangerously close to sacrilege.

As a result of recent newspaper articles by Chebeague Island journalist Donna Damon, hundreds of motivated Mainers were itching for a fight. While a "Save Our Pilot Cracker" petition was being circulated, outraged Maine cracker lovers flooded the Nabisco Customer Comment Hotline seeking to avert this miscarriage of culinary justice before it was too late.

As battle lines were being drawn, could I simply stand by and do nothing? What was I going to tell my grandkids when they asked, "Where were you when they tried to take away our Pilot Crackers?" Fortunately, one phone call to my CBS *Sunday Morning* producer Mary

Lou Teel was all it took to bring the cavalry charging up from New York City with lights blazing and cameras whirring.

My crew barely had their gear set up before the normally reserved Chebeague islanders began cueing up to vent their frustration before a TV audience of several million. One fellow even sang us a hastily composed anthem (to the tune of "My Bonny Lies Over The Ocean") with his neighbors chiming in on the chorus—*briiiiing, back! . . . briiiiing back! My Pilot crackers to me!*

We even managed to film a chowder cracker history lesson and cooking demonstration in the Islesboro farmhouse kitchen of celebrated food historian and *New York Times* best selling author Sandy Oliver.

In the final scene, I stood at the Chebeague Island public boat landing and voiced the question that was on everyone's mind: "Will a small group of Maine islanders be able to stay the hand of a mighty multinational corporation?" Then I added, "I wouldn't bet against the Mainers!"

I certainly got that one right! Our story sparked a huge outpouring of response from across the country. Several million folks, most of whom had never even heard of Pilot Crackers until that very moment, tuned in and apparently a fair percentage of them jumped on the Save the Pilot Cracker bandwagon.

When the *New York Times* picked up the story the following day, I knew the tide had turned. At a press conference a week or so later, a Nabisco spokesperson officially threw in the towel citing "that Tim Sample Postcard on CBS Sunday Morning" as a primary factor in their decision to keep the Crown Pilot Cracker on the shelf. Awesome!

We even shot a follow up Postcard featuring the Nabisco P.R. flacks (don't tell me these guys don't recognize a marketing opportunity when they see one) loading commemorative boxes of Pilot Crackers onto a Casco Bay Lines ferry for the voyage to Portland and grand "re-introduction" festivities at DiMillo's floating restaurant.

So in the end did I really save the Pilot Cracker as June had hoped? Well, yes and no. I certainly helped give the venerable old wafer a "last hurrah." But sadly, after a few years passed and the crowds had thinned out, Nabisco quietly shut down the production line.

Hey, that's OK. For well over a century the Crown Pilot Cracker survived in humble obscurity in the cupboards and pantries of New England. Then, thanks to a handful of die-hard fans and a sympathetic CBS reporter it left the stage in a blaze of glory.

To Boldly Go . . .

To Boldly Go . . .

I was a young, wet-behind-the-ears, illustrator/cartoonist, barely 27 years old in 1978 when I moved into Noel Stookey's guest house in South Blue Hill, Maine, to begin what I then hoped would be a successful career in animation.

I had met Noel (the Paul of Peter, Paul and Mary) about two years earlier when I was an opening act for him at what is now Merrill Auditorium in Portland. Over the next couple years we continued to perform together, gradually discovering that we had a lot of things in common besides music, including a lifelong interest in cartoon animation.

Although I'd been a fan of Noel's since the early 60s, I'd only recently learned that he was also a talented cartoonist with a knack for generating funny voices and whacky sound effects. That's a good skill set for an animator. In fact, in 1968, working with Warner Brothers, Noel had helped create a cartoon based on the PP&M song "Norman Normal" (yes kids, you can watch it on YouTube.) The animated short feature, loosely based on the song of the same name, had been shown in movie theatres around the world. Color me impressed.

Noel and I began daydreaming about starting our own animation studio and before long a plan began to take shape. The next thing I remember I was in South Blue Hill building an animation studio with Noel and a few other talented, ambitious, and incredibly naïve young artists.

We managed to scrape together some used equipment, including a large cel-duplicating machine once used by Walt Disney, and began setting up shop on the second floor of a refurbished henhouse overlooking Blue Hill Bay. Noel's dad, Nick, a retired machinist and inventor, built us a professional-grade animation stand using about a hundred-and-fifty bucks worth of grommets, nuts, bolts, and PVC pipe from the local hardware store. Thus outfitted with second-hand gear, a homemade animation stand, and a shoestring budget, Neworld Animation was born!

Our first paying job involved creating a 59-second TV spot featuring original "full cel" animation. Now, 59 seconds doesn't sound like a lot of time to fill until you discover that each second of on-screen animation contains around two dozen painstakingly drawn, inked, and colored frames. That's more than 1400 frames per minute, plus another 1400 frames for the "pencil test" to make sure the movement looks right before you ink it in. Did I mention writing the script, recording the sound track, designing and painting the backgrounds? Hmmm, suddenly, running our very own animation studio was starting to feel an awful lot like working in our very own coal mine.

Fortunately, Stookey's celebrity status brought plenty of interesting visitors by to break up the monotony. One day Noel showed up with a fellow named Doug who asked intelligent questions and mentioned that if any of us were coming to Los Angeles we should stop in and see *his* current animation project.

Since I was, in fact, going to be in L.A. myself in a couple of weeks he gave me his card and told me to call when I was in town. Sure enough, finding myself with a little extra time on my hands I gave Doug a call. He gave me an address and the following morning I dropped by. Frankly, I wasn't too impressed. Our funky old henhouse in Maine was pretty cool compared to a grungy warehouse in the industrial quarter of Long Beach. Oh well, I guess things are tough when you're just starting out.

When I rang the buzzer a man with a headset appeared and opened the door. Stepping inside, it took me a second to absorb what I was looking at. Dozens of technicians sat at illuminated consoles maneuvering little motorized cameras along a vast network of tracks snaking through the building. Suspended from invisible wires in the center of the warehouse I saw…The Starship *Enterprise*!

It turned out that Doug, who had dropped by to visit our little animation studio in Maine, was in fact legendary special effects genius Douglas Trumbull, whose credits included *2001: A Space Odyssey* and *Close Encounters of the Third Kind*. The scene being shot that morning was for *Star Trek: The Motion Picture.*

I've always figured that if you aren't embarrassed on a regular basis, you simply aren't paying attention. So, my mortification at having failed to recognize one of Hollywood's most famous special effects geniuses was short lived. On the other hand, the memory of spending an entire day watching a true Hollywood legend create movie magic in an old warehouse? I expect that will last a lifetime.

Naming the Band

In my opinion, everyone on the planet ought to start a garage band at least once. This has nothing to do with music—we *are* after all talking about *garage bands*. Rather, it concerns a time honored adolescent rite of passage requiring no musical talent whatsoever. I'm referring of course to that sacred teenage ritual known as "Naming the Band."

Having come of age in the 60s, arguably the golden age of band names, I know whereof I speak. After all I once helped name a band "Muzak" (we folded relatively quickly, thereby avoiding copyright lawsuits). Decades later I witnessed the birth of my stepson Ben's awesomely named garage band, "Steaming Pile."

Oddly enough, it would seem that truly creative band naming is a fairly recent phenomenon. In the 1940s big-band music was hip but band names were square as a cardboard box. The Glenn Miller Band, The Tommy Dorsey Band, The Duke Ellington Orchestra, the list is almost endless. While the music kept folks up dancing all night, the band names were strictly from Snoozeville.

Fortunately, 1950s doo-wop bands moved the bar up a notch, or at least towed it out of that eponymous ditch. Exotic bird names were in vogue and The Penguins, The Orioles, and The Flamingoes all had Top 40 hits. Folks who wandered away from the aviary adopted a more onomatopoetic style, characterized by the smooth, swishy sibilant sounds of bands named The Chiffons and The Channels. Despite the colorful names however, doo-wop groups continued to begin band names with a 1940s style "The."

Clearly, this habit of starting band names with "The" was tough to break. Well into the 1960s, bands were still struggling with it. Virtually all the early British Invasion bands arrived with such traditional construction: The Beatles, The Rolling Stones, The Animals, etc.

Occasionally a band would try dropping "The" only to have their adoring fans pick it up and glue it back on. Pete Townsend's cleverly named Who had barely smashed their first amplifier when "The" got attached and they've been cashing checks made out to The Who ever since.

If memory serves (no guarantee of that at my age), the first 60s band to arrive without a "The" moniker was Herman's Hermits. Then, before you could say "What's your sign?", band names without a "The" were everywhere. Steppenwolf and Buffalo Springfield come to mind. These bands managed to convey that all-important yet elusive 60s hipness while simultaneously rebuffing all attempts to attach a "The" to them.

Nonsense names like Moby Grape, Ultimate Spinach, and Strawberry Alarm Clock made a brief appearance in the 60s as well, but vanished nearly as quickly as they'd arrived, falling out of favor around the same time young rockers figured out that the "brilliant" spiritual insights revealed while under the influence of recreational chemicals rarely shone as brightly in the harsh light of day.

Many a crestfallen flower child awakened to discover that the words "buy more Clorox," scrawled in crayon across the bathroom mirror at the pinnacle of the previous night's revelry were, alas, not the secret of existence after all.

Which brings me to the progressive rock bands of the late 60s, whose string infested, quasi-symphonic music and abstract lyrics at least implied that there might be a deep spiritual secret in there someplace. A good example of this genre, sporting one of the most excellent band names of all time, was Procol Harum.

Perhaps you're wondering how a bunch of 60s Brit rockers stumbled upon the name Procol Harum. I hadn't thought too much about it until I heard a recent newscast claiming that the name Procol Harum, currently attached to some Jihadi terrorist outfit, actually means "western education is sinful" or words to that effect.

I was appalled! But, a few minutes online set things straight. Apparently the aforementioned terrorists actually call themselves "Boko Haram"—similar sounding, yet a completely uncool band name in this or any other era. Whew! That was close.

So if this iconic 1960s rock band wasn't actually saying "western education is sinful" how did they get the name Procol Harum?

You may have noticed that, like our friends in the legal profession, newspaper columnists tend to ask questions only if and when we already know the answers. So here's the scoop.

According to the band's pianist, Gary Booker, the founding band members, having rejected every name they could think of, experienced a classic "garage band moment" and decided to name the band Procol Harum, after a cat owned by a friend of their manager. And that, boys and girls, is how legendary rock bands *really* get their names.

Autographs

I was returning a car at the Hertz kiosk in the tiny boutique airport in Missoula, Montana, recently when the lady behind the counter glanced down at my name on the rental agreement, did a double take, and asked if I was that guy from TV. Following a full confession on my part she asked if I'd give her my autograph—my compliance sparking a minor chain reaction involving some elderly CBS *Sunday Morning* fans from Denver standing in line behind me.

Encounters of this sort happen with far less frequency these days than they did back when I was working at the network. I suspect that the fact that they happen at all is mostly because, in the digital age, images of any sort never seem to disappear completely. These days it seems that every scrap of film or video ever shot has acquired the half-life of plutonium, residing in a "cloud" somewhere and instantly accessible via endless billions of laptops, smart phones, and iPads.

Some sixteen hours after departing from Montana, my wife and I arrived in Portland only to discover that in our absence a fuse in the box outside the house had blown, shutting down half our electrical circuits, including the one for our refrigerator/freezer. Welcome home Mr. and Mrs. Sample. Your vacation is now officially over.

The next morning, groggy and a bit cranky from lack of sleep, we contacted a local electrician. Quickly diagnosing the problem he located a replacement part, made the repair, and presented us with a bill for services rendered. As we were preparing to pay up he announced that he was a "huge fan," cheerfully handed over the defective breaker (about three pounds of corroded metal and faded plastic), and asked if I'd mind autographing it for him. Sure, why not?

After he'd left I found myself ruminating on the topic of autographs in general, which when you really think about it are a pretty odd phenomenon. I mean, in what trophy case, exactly, does one display a signed Hertz Rent-a-Car brochure or a worn out electrical circuit breaker autographed in felt tip marker by an aging Maine humorist?

The value of an autograph is of course entirely contingent upon the perceived fame and/or notoriety of the person doing the signing. The bold, almost calligraphic, signature style favored by one particular signer of our Declaration of Independence, for example, has gained such iconic status that folks routinely refer to the signing of a legal document as "putting your John Hancock on it."

So, for the genuinely famous an autograph carries obvious cachet in that "brush with greatness" sort of way. My friend Dave over in New Hampshire has a massive collection of sports and entertainment memorabilia, including an authentic 1966 poster of The Beatles at Shea Stadium actually signed by John, Paul, George, and Ringo. Impressive!

And who wouldn't get goose bumps holding a baseball signed by sports legend George "Babe" Ruth. I'll even admit to having collected a few autographs over the years myself. Once while sitting at a gate in the Phoenix airport, I heard a familiar voice on a nearby cell phone. When the speaker finished I introduced myself and came away with a scrap of paper signed by Senator John McCain.

But, what about those of us stuck on the lower rungs of the celebrity ladder? I'm thinking of an incident many years ago when I was visiting a sick friend at a Lewiston hospital. Apparently some of the nurses on his floor were fans of mine so I ended up signing a few autographs. One fellow though, a male nurse recently transferred from New Jersey, didn't get it. Having no clue as to why anybody would want *my* autograph, he simply walked up to me and popped the question, "Are you famous or something?"

How do you answer a question like that? "Well," I replied, " I suppose that depends on who you ask." Pondering my response he turned and walked away.

A half hour later, as I was heading out the front door, I noticed Mr. New Jersey RN striding purposefully in my direction. Catching up with me he thrust a ballpoint pen and some paper into my hand and requested an autograph.

"But, I thought you'd never heard of me. Why would you want my autograph?"

"Well," he replied, "I'm still not sure whether you're really famous or not but I figured I'd better get an autograph just in case you were."

Who can argue with logic like that? I took the offered pen and paper and proceeded to give my first and probably last "just-in-case-you-turn-out-to-be-famous" backup autograph.

Passing Venues

I spend a lot of time driving around the back roads of New England and lately I've caught myself mentally updating an informal inventory I seem to be keeping of venues I've performed at over the years. Whether cruising past some opera house in New Hampshire, a hotel in Boston, or a college campus in Vermont's Northeast Kingdom, I find myself thinking, "Hey didn't I play there back in . . .?"

Although I still occasionally perform at some of these places, a disconcerting number of them have simply vanished. Others, while still standing, have long since retired from show biz.

Driving through Kingfield last spring I noticed someone sweeping the sidewalk in front of the old Herbert Hotel. Seeing that venerable old pile again stimulated a flood of memories and I was momentarily transported back to a long, cold winter in the mid-1970s. I recall spending a lot of evenings at The Herbert that winter. In fact my real life experiences in its basement lounge inspired my routine "The Dubious Brothers vs. The Skidder Crowd," a remarkably true-to-life chronicle of the adventures my band mates and I shared while performing at The Herbert.

People are often surprised to learn that The Dubious Brothers was an actual band with a rotating roster of players, including pianist Stephen Bither of The Wicked Good Band, saxophone player Richie Gerber (Howard Stern's real life "Cousin Richie"), and my best friend and songwriting partner from high school Bill Arsenault and his younger brother Ron (the *original* dubious brothers) on various guitars. We played regularly at The Herbert and, while consistently failing to connect with the upscale Volvo driving "ski crowd," we certainly managed to run head-on into the "skidder crowd."

The day I stopped by, the owners offered me a free nostalgia tour of the downstairs lounge, currently serving as a storage room for unused restaurant equipment. Under a thick layer of dust and cobwebs, the place looked eerily similar to the way it did when we last played there circa 1976.

I'll admit to getting a few goose bumps as I wandered around the former Hogpenny Lounge recalling those bygone days when a gig meant lugging hundreds of pounds of bulky amps and PA systems up and down narrow flights of stairs and playing "45 on 15 off" until the wee hours of the morning.

The patrons of The Hogpenny Lounge back then weren't likely to be sipping martinis and discussing stock options. They were, in fact, an almost exclusively male, hard drinking, loud and rowdy, bar bourbon bunch not much prone to small talk. But, it was a gig and as I recall it paid nearly $50 a night!

Fortunately, a very different sort of venue from that era, The Grand Theatre in Ellsworth, is still alive and well.

My history at The Grand (a.k.a. The Hancock County Auditorium) spans thirty-plus years and my family's connection goes even further back than that. My mom, born and raised in nearby Brooklin, tells of childhood trips to Ellsworth to watch movies there in the 1930s.

I've lost track of the number of times I've performed there, sharing the stage with a host of great performers, including folkies like Noel Stookey and Tom Paxton, storytellers Marshall Dodge, Robert Bryan, Joe Perham, Kendall Morse, and John MacDonald, and many more. I once narrated an original Maine humor version of "Peter and the Wolf" with The Bangor Symphony at The Grand.

Of course no trip down Memory Lane is complete without a stop at The Opera House at Boothbay Harbor, simply because it's where my life onstage really began. Back in the 1960s it was still the Pythian Opera House. That's where I saw my very first live play, a local amateur theater group production of *Gramercy Ghost*, sometime in the late 50s. I sat in the audience at Opera House talent shows watching Brud Pierce play the spoons and around 1966, as a nervous teenager, I stood behind the curtain waiting to make my rock 'n' roll debut in a local "battle of the bands" on that same Opera House stage.

Memory, of course can play tricks and I'm aware that many of mine benefit from the strange alchemy embodied in the old saying, "Tragedy plus time equals comedy."

A case in point: Following one show many years ago, I was approached by an elderly man asking me to autograph two ticket stubs. I happily complied, feeling like a big shot until he turned to leave and I overheard him telling his wife, "I can get fifty cents for these at a yard sale!"

A Great Audience

Following a recent after-dinner speaking engagement, I mentioned to a friend that the group (150 or so Registered Maine Guides) had been "a great audience." "Oh," she said. "Are some audiences better than others?"

According to an old show biz adage, "There's no such thing as a bad audience . . . only bad entertainers." But forty-plus years onstage has me drawing a different conclusion. While I agree that it's a lot easier to blame the audience than it is to take responsibility for your own shortcomings, experience has also taught me that some audiences are, in fact, significantly better than others.

To be successful in my line of work, you need to develop the knack of quickly and accurately "reading the room." Once you've figured that out, you'll have a much better shot at adapting your material and delivery to the specific personality of each new audience you encounter.

As odd as it may be to imagine hundreds of separate individuals sharing a single personality, from where I stand (behind the microphone), that's exactly how it feels.

With that in mind, here are some audience types I've met over the years:

Go Ahead, Try To Make Me Laugh: Fortunately an extremely rare animal, this audience can occasionally be found in a super-hip urban comedy club environment. Although most folks would agree that the whole point of going out and listening to a comedian is to enjoy a few good laughs, that's certainly not the case with this crowd. They seem to take a perverse pride in their ability to sit sphinx-like through an entire evening of hilarious comedy without cracking a smile.

Almost exclusively young, frequently male, and competitive to the point of being combative, I suspect that members of this audience would also qualify for inclusion in that microscopic demographic, "People most likely to challenge Mike Tyson to a bar fight." Not a fun bunch.

Oh, Is There Somebody Onstage Talking?: Like just about everybody in show business, the early years of my career were spent in venues where the patrons had at least 27 different reasons for being there, each of them far more important than listening to me.

Those reasons included getting drunk, meeting their drug dealer, getting drunk *with* their drug dealer, watching baseball, football, basketball etc., on the big screen TV, and of course "The Three Ps"—Pinball, Pugilism, and Procreation. It's likely that an audience of this type inspired the song lyric, "If I can make it there, I'll make it anywhere."

The Nervous Nellies: Self-consciousness and humor, like oil and water, are incapable of occupying the same space at the same time. One of them inevitably must displace the other.

A marvelous side effect of laughter, of course, is the spontaneous break it gives us from our daily grind (hence the phrase "comic relief"). Laughter suddenly, almost magically, displaces the stress of day-to-day life, instantly filling the void with a pleasant wave of endorphins. Ahhhhh, that's better.

Sadly, an audience composed of people unable or unwilling to relinquish their self-consciousness is an audience virtually incapable of laughter. If there's a physical epicenter of all human self-consciousness I'm betting it's located in a high school somewhere, since for many of us, high school was the high-water mark of self-consciousness.

Perhaps it's no surprise then that the toughest audience I ever encountered was made up entirely of recent high school graduates and their parents packed into a stuffy gym on a college campus during freshman orientation week. Brutal!

The Co-worker Cohort: This is by far my favorite corporate audience. The secret is that the individual audience members are genuinely comfortable being around each other. Laughter, like crying, is an involuntary emotional response, so there's a certain amount of trust and emotional vulnerability involved when laughing with others.

Since people in the helping professions, such as nurses, social workers, teachers, EMTs, and CNAs, inhabit a work environment where trust and emotional honesty are part of the job description, they make a fantastic audience, always happy to swap their job related stress for some laugh generated endorphins.

The True Blue Fans: This is every performer's favorite audience. There's only one reason they're sitting out there waiting for the curtain to open. They came to see you! I never feel the need to *make* this audience laugh. They *came* to laugh. They *want* to laugh. Give them half a chance and they'll be rolling in the aisles.

Getting this audience laughing is a lot like torching that big old bonfire on homecoming weekend. All I really have to do is set a match to it, step back, and bask in the warm familiar glow.

I'll See You on the Radio

I love radio. Of course, being a baby boomer who hit puberty just as the British Invasion hit American airwaves explains a lot. The invasion I'm referring to involved a handful of young English musicians with names like John, Paul, George, and Ringo who, sometime around 1964, ventured across the pond seeking nothing more complicated than to hold our hand. By the end of the decade, of course, they practically owned the place.

Nowadays aging Brit rock stars like to recount tales of late nights spent listening to broadcasts from Radio Luxemburg playing the latest hits from American rockers like Elvis Presley and Jerry Lee Lewis.

As a freshly minted teenager (I turned thirteen in '64), I had my own version of that ritual. My Radio Luxemburg was a fuzzy, AM signal from WBZ Radio in Boston. Apparently, after sundown, the AM signal (remember children, this was in that twilight time just after the dinosaurs and just before FM) got cranked up really high so that even distant Mainers could tune in.

WBZ arrived in my teenage bedroom via the tiny speaker (or optional wired earpiece for private listening) in a matchbook-size Panasonic transistor radio I'd won selling magazine subscriptions. Before long, just like John and Paul and all the rest, I, too, was feverishly scheming to get on the radio.

My big break came when WBZ held a jingle-writing contest. I just needed to write a short jingle extolling the fabulousness of my favorite station, call said station, sing the jingle into the phone, then sit back and wait for fame to arrive.

The part about writing the jingle was easy. By virtue of being thirteen I was possessed of that bizarre overconfidence born of youthful innocence, boundless energy, and a dearth of real life experience, which insists that "You can do anything if you put your mind to it." An hour or so later I had my jingle. I'd written the lyrics on a Big Chief pad and, lacking a tape recorder, simply sung the tune enough times to burn the melody

43

deep into the canyons of my cerebral cortex. The next day I called in and sang it into a tape recorder.

Do I remember the song? Sure. But that doesn't mean I'm going to share it with you. Anyway, although I never forgot the jingle (hint: it was an up tempo ditty with a vaguely "Latin" beat, easy to dance to), I did temporarily forget the contest. When WBZ didn't call the very next morning I moved on to more pressing matters like lining up a cute girl to help me with my math homework.

A couple of weeks later I came home from school to find a package addressed to me from WBZ Radio, Soldiers Field Road, Boston, Massachusetts. My eyeballs fell out and steam blasted from both my ears! I tore it open and found a brand new Polaroid camera! I won't even bother trying to explain the magic of instant Polaroid photography to the iPhone generation. Trust me. You had to be there. Plus, the real prize was a letter saying I'd won the contest. They were going to play my jingle on WBZ!

Honestly, I can't remember what happened next. I just know I felt dazed in a way that I imagine those hapless housewives on *Queen for a Day*, a quiz show of the era, must have felt when they were temporarily lifted out of grinding poverty, showered with washers, dryers, color TVs, chest freezers, and the like (ouch!), and then presumably driven home in a limo and dropped at the curb back in the old neighborhood.

I'm not sure whether the letter explained when to listen or I just listened every chance I got. Either way, I'll never forget the thrill of hearing my own voice coming out of a radio speaker for the very first time. It was, as they say now, a "transformational moment." Hey, everybody! That's me on the radio!

That was my first radio experience, but far from my last. I eventually got my own radio show and almost twenty years after hearing my jingle, I made the first of many appearances on *The Larry Glick Show*. Glick was a giant of New England radio and one of my personal heroes. As I rode the elevator to the broadcast studio on the top floor of the WBZ building at Soldiers Field Road, Boston, Massachusetts, I could almost hear my teenage voice singing a faintly calypso tune that went something like this, "All of the people in old Bean Town are tuned to the happiest sounds around . . . WBZ!"

My Fabulous Movie Career

There are worse places to shoot a feature film than Maine in the summer. When I was a kid, locals, tourists, and summer people alike would cue up at the Strand theatre for the annual screening of the movie adaptation of Rodgers and Hammerstein's Broadway hit *Carousel*, featuring scenes shot in and around our home town as well as the occasional friend, neighbor, or relative who'd managed to get work as an extra. "Hey everybody, there's Aunt Martha at the clambake!" Big stuff.

So, back in the 80s, when approached by director Richard Searles about appearing in his latest film, I jumped at the opportunity. After all, Searles's oeuvre included such award winning filmed-in-Maine documentaries as *Dead River Rough Cut* and *Trap Day on Monhegan*. Heck, he'd even recruited an all-star Maine cast for the film. How could I go wrong with co-stars such as Senator Edmund Muskie and Olympic Gold Medalist Joanie Benoit?

Huh? Who? Yeah, that's right. If I hadn't been dazzled by notions of stardom it might have dawned on me, as it has no doubt dawned on you, that my fellow actors, although high profile public figures, were not actually real actors in the sense of being people who know how to act—a critical distinction as it turned out.

In fact, the only cast member with anything like a genuine Hollywood resume was the lovely and talented Katherine "Kay Aldrich" Tucker, a lively and lovely lady with genuine star quality whom I first met at the pre-production cast party she hosted in her gracious home overlooking Camden Harbor. Back in the 1940s Ms. Tucker had managed to parlay her success as a top rated fashion model into a film career in Hollywood. She'd even done a screen test for the roll of Scarlett O'Hara in *Gone with the Wind*! Also, it didn't hurt that she still owned an immaculate chauffeur-driven 1930s vintage Rolls Royce touring car, which would come in handy in one of the important scenes.

And what sort of scene might that be? Ah, I was afraid you'd ask. Given the director's reputation for award-winning documentaries you probably assumed that's the sort of film I was in. Sadly, no. In fact, my genius director friend had decided to break that mold completely and veer off in a wildly different direction. The film, a comedy envisioned as a "light hearted romp," emerged from the cutting room utterly devoid of humor. It was, in fact, an unmitigated disaster. He should have stuck with the documentaries.

You've perhaps noticed that thus far I've managed to cleverly avoid divulging the actual title of the movie. If it's all the same to you, I'd just as soon keep it that way. "Bad" doesn't even begin to cover this flick. I can't even claim that it's one of those campy "so bad it's good" movies like Ed Wood's immortal, unintentionally hysterical, *Plan 9 from Outer Space*. Nope this one's just a plain old-fashioned bomb, a first rate P-U stinker.

Mercifully, very few people have actually seen this picture. It certainly never played in a real movie theatre. Technically, I believe the industry term for a film like this is "straight to video," only in this case it was more like "straight to the 99-cent bin at Marden's," and from there it went directly to the landfill.

I'd pretty much blocked any conscious memory of the debacle until I made the mistake of regaling my eldest daughter with a few hilarious tales of bygone days, including my summer as a would-be movie star. Her curiosity was sparked. Though she didn't have many details to work with, it turns out you don't need that many details when you have an hour or two and Google on your laptop. Anyway, she managed to locate and purchase a VHS copy in that vast garbage heap of human folly known as the Internet and after suffering through the first few excruciating minutes, passed it along to me as, what? A memento? A keepsake? An albatross to hang around my neck?

I survived the humiliation and probably still have it buried somewhere in the garage. I certainly can't imagine I'd have unleashed it on some poor unsuspecting shopper at the local Goodwill. Wherever it is I hope it stays there forever. I certainly won't be watching it anytime soon. And with any luck you won't either.

Spring Water Evangelist

Awhile back I got a call from the folks at the Poland Spring Water Company. They needed some help correcting a serious misunderstanding in certain parts of the U.S. regarding their product. Like any Maine school kid, I knew the legend of the pure, healthy mineral water that flowed from a mysterious spring in Maine. The stuff was so famous they named a whole town after it! But somehow people living in exotic far-away places with strange sounding names like Chicago, Detroit, and Minneapolis tended to associate Poland Spring Water with, of all things, Poland! Not Poland, Maine, but Poland the country in Europe! The company figured that I was just the fella to set 'em straight. My mission was to carry the message that the true source of this marvelous water, although still a well kept secret, was a lot closer to Kennebunk than to Krakow.

A tour was organized by their New York ad agency with my first appearance scheduled for the Mall of America in Bloomington, Minnesota. Arriving a day early, I spent the first night in the town of Owatonna, where I chanced upon a water fountain honoring the Native American Princess Owatonna. It was a rusty, slightly mildewed cast iron affair offering an unappealing trickle of what a bronze plaque assured me was "World Famous Owatonna Water." One tentative sip convinced me that Poland Spring Water stood an excellent chance of drubbing the home team this time out.

And so it did. The Mall of America event was an unqualified success. Hundreds of weary shoppers gathered around our stage-prop Maine Cabin swilling free bottles of Poland Spring water as I regaled them with humorous Maine stories. Our next stop was Chicago's Union Station. Did I mention that this entire dog and pony show was being staged at considerable cost by a big New York advertising agency? Venues were determined by consulting complex demographic data, which is exactly how they picked Union Station, with an "audience" consisting of some 50,000-plus folks a day for two days. That's over 100,000 potential customers! The way they pitched it, it sounded like The Beatles playing Shea Stadium. Not quite.

While their data was accurate, those agency bean counters hadn't considered one important fact. Unlike the happy, relaxed shoppers at the Mall of America, these throngs would be made up of commuters headed someplace else as quickly as humanly possible. Not exactly my idea of an attentive audience. I could see that using the Mall of America approach, except with the audience changing thirty times during a ten-minute monologue, was a recipe for disaster. Unless I thought of something else, I was quite possibly facing the longest sixteen hours of my career.

The situation was this: for the next two eight-hour days I'd be standing outside a rustic "Maine Cabin" in the middle of Union Station, in a blue blazer and khaki slacks, holding a microphone, jostled by harried commuters walking at breakneck speed. Clearly, even a half hour of this would be pure torture. Then it hit me. What would people expect me to be doing in a situation like that? Of course, I'd be there to interview people! So, microphone in hand, I waded out into the stream of commuters and started asking questions. Presently a small crowd of curious onlookers gathered to see what the fuss was about. Not in quite so big a rush, these folks assumed that a man with a microphone meant there must be a TV camera somewhere nearby, right? Nope. There was no TV, no radio, not even a tape recorder. But I'd solved my biggest problem simply by getting folks to stop and pay attention. Now I just needed some interview questions.

As a correspondent for CBS News *Sunday Morning* I'd gained enough credibility as "the guy from Maine" to sound plausible asking questions like, "Have you ever been to Maine?" and "What's the first thing you think of when I say Maine?" Besides the obvious connection to the free Poland Spring water we were handing out, I had accidentally stumbled on a rare opportunity to do my own "market research" on Midwesterners' opinions about Maine. Their responses were both surprising and fascinating.

For example, when asked which word occurred to them when I said Maine, the most common response was "green." OK, didn't exactly expect that one. Many thought Maine was "close to New York" (not likely chummy), or perhaps a Canadian province. Some responses could have been generated by the Maine Department of Tourism. Folks considered Maine "a nice place to live," "quiet," and even "friendly." That last one surprised me given our reputation for dishing out cranky one-liners to summer visitors. Speaking of which, many proudly quoted the "You cahhn't get there from here" line from the original *Bert and I* recording as if it were our state motto.

Besides clearing up some of my sponsor's "image problems" in that neck of the woods I had a great learning experience. There was, however, one poignant note. I was surprised at the number of Midwesterners who confessed a secret desire to someday retire and spend their golden years running a little country store in Maine. I didn't have the heart to tell them that there are plenty of '"little country store" owners here in Maine who'd be more than happy to take their hard earned cash, turn over the keys and retire themselves, perhaps to a quite little town in, oh I don't know, how about Minnesota?

Lights, Camera . . . Lobsters!

Early in my career a reporter asked me whether I had "a background in show business." I'll admit the question threw me for a loop. I couldn't offer the sort of stories you read in the supermarket tabloids. You know, where it turns out George Clooney's aunt was Rosemary Clooney. Uh huh. That explains a lot! Unable to shake any movie stars out of my family tree I was forced to look elsewhere.

Did winning a prize speaking contest in high school count? Not to anybody who was paying attention. Ditto for the teenage rock bands. Still, I kept thinking there must have been something about those years growing up on the Maine coast that conjured visions of footlights, opening nights, big breaks, and rave reviews. Then it struck me. When I was a kid it seemed like the whole town was one big theatrical production! In fact, I had a ringside seat for our annual transformation from a quiet fishing village where nothing much happens to a world-class vacation destination teeming with gawking throngs of paying customers.

Here's how it works. Imagine that the cast and crew of this show have somehow managed to survive another long, cold, dark off-season. Then spring finally arrives and everybody gets busy. Times-a-wastin' folks! There are signs to paint, flyers to print and distribute, posters to design. Everything has to be cleaned up, spit-shined, and ready before the big opening. The actors will need to be fitted for costumes and start memorizing their lines. What actors you say? Well, the shopkeepers, tour boat captains, information booth volunteers, parking lot attendants, tow truck operators, waitresses, and bus boys of course. Basically the "cast" is anybody who will be interacting directly with the "audience" (that throng of tourists I mentioned). Whether a star or a crowd scene extra, everybody knows that the success of the season depends on the show coming off without a hitch and we've only got three months to make twelve months' worth of income so every day counts! That goes for the roadies and tech crew as well. Even great actors can't save a show if the lighting is terrible, the props are cheesy, and the a/v system has a blown fuse. So, we'll need all our plumbers, electricians, painters, and carpenters on deck and ready for work.

"What if I don't work in the tourism industry?" you ask. Hey, if you're going to be on the set you'll still need to follow the rules. Getting groceries during "tourist season"? You should defer to the paying "audience" as much as possible. Pick off-hours for your shopping and if you must drive use short cuts and back roads that the tourists aren't familiar with. Always stay backstage and don't disturb the audience! If you're a fisherman, just go about your business as if you weren't being constantly filmed and posted on YouTube. You are an important part of the set. Occasionally you may even get a line or two of dialogue. For instance, if a tourist asks you "Does this road go all the way to Portland?" feel free to reply, "Don't go nowhere mistah, it just sits there." Just make sure that you keep the crankiness at a low simmer. We need good reviews, always keeping in mind that our season is shockingly brief. We really only have from July 4th to Labor Day to make a good impression and rake in some hard currency. The weeks between Memorial Day and July 4th are more like the "off-Broadway" run. We get to rewrite the script, polish the tunes, and refine the dance steps before an actual live audience. But, that doesn't change the fact that the big opening is always July 4th week-end.

From July 4th to Labor Day it's all giddy pandemonium and hard work. Then, suddenly it's Labor Day. The audience evaporates like ground fog in the morning sun and after sweeping up all those crumpled lobster bibs and discarded taffy wrappers, we pour a cup of coffee and sit down to count the season's box office receipts. "How'd your summer go?" "Not too shabby considerin' the rain we had in July." "Ayuh, well, there's always next year." Ah, yes, next year. And that, my friends, is what I call "show biz."

III

You Live Here Year 'Round

For Pilgrim Feet

Independence Day is that marvelously homemade celebration of liberty, reflecting the unique values and sensibilities of small town America. Oh sure, big cities have celebrations, too, but if you can set aside your political cynicism long enough to experience the kind of heartfelt patriotic pride and genuine optimism that, against all odds, still runs like a spring-fed stream through the landscape of contemporary American life, I'd recommend spending the Fourth in a small Maine town.

Having grown up in just such a place back in the 1950s and 60s, my earliest memories of July 4th celebrations conjure up an increasingly hard-to-imagine era when gift shops were few and far between and fishing boats, a massive seafood processing plant, and busy shipyards dominated the local waterfront.

My childhood home still sits on a hill overlooking the harbor. Although the view these days is obscured by more than a half-century's worth of tree growth, back then, on a clear day, I could see Monhegan Island from my bedroom window. Despite this enviable view, we *always* walked downtown when it was time for the fireworks show to start.

Who could blame us? There's just something magical about standing on the town dock at sunset with your siblings, the mailman, a stray dog or two, your first grade teacher and her husband, and everybody else packed in tighter than sardines in a can, anxiously anticipating that first whistling contrail rising into the night sky, arcing toward its spectacular "bombs bursting in air" payoff!

Speaking of bombs bursting in air, July 4th remains the one day of the year when you will absolutely be expected to sing all six verses of "America The Beautiful" from memory, including the one with the unlikely reference to feet:

> Oh beautiful for Pilgrim feet
> Whose stern impassioned stress
> A thoroughfare for freedom beat
> Across the wildernesssss . . .

You gotta love that one. Besides the quirky foot reference, catchy tune, patriotic theme, and awesome rhyming, you get a couple of new vocabulary words tossed in at no extra charge.

In my professional life I've been privileged to participate in plenty of memorable small town Maine July 4th events. Have you ever been to Brooks, Maine? Brooks is a tiny Waldo County town with an amazingly big spirit. The year I performed there the whole 4th of July show was staged at the gravel pit and I think all of the 1000 or so residents showed up. The big draw was a local long-haul trucker with several million miles in his rear view mirror, giving guided tours of the cab of his brand new 18-wheeler. Before you start snickering, have you ever been inside one of those rigs? It's a fascinating experience, one you're not likely to duplicate in New York or L.A.

These days I like to spend July 4th in Washington County. A couple years ago I performed at Grand Lake Stream with some local acts, including my old friend Randy Spencer, the Singing Registered Maine Guide, who really got the crowd going with an original tune everybody could relate to, "The Black Fly Blues."

My wife and I have also watched the Lubec 4th of July parade from our friend Vikki's front lawn. Lubec is about an hour's drive from our place in South Princeton and although the actual parade only lasted fifteen minutes that year, everybody was having such a good time that when they returned to the starting point they decided to keep going and do the whole circuit one more time. See what I mean about "homemade"? Naturally, the cheers were even louder the second time around.

Perhaps my favorite Independence Day memory ever is from 1986, when I was Grand Marshall of Eastport's Annual Callithumpian Fourth of July Parade. That year marked the 100th anniversary of the installation of the Statue of Liberty in New York harbor. Millions of dollars had been donated by private citizens toward restoration of the iconic landmark in time for her centennial.

Since the project had received a lot of press, I wasn't surprised to spot a young girl marching along, covered in tin foil, holding aloft a cardboard torch. I was, however, baffled to note that her tin foil costume was almost entirely obscured by an intricate network of plastic soda straws painstakingly scotch-taped together.

The mystery was solved when their mom explained that her daughter had insisted on the elaborate overlay of straws, meant to represent the metal construction staging, an integral part of Miss Liberty for the entire span of this young girl's life. Ah, I thought, of course. God Bless America!

Celebrating Adversity

As often as possible, my wife and I try to spend Memorial Day weekend at our camp in Washington County. If we're lucky the sun will be out. But, whether it is or not, the black flies certainly will be, although I've noticed recently that the mosquitoes seem to be waging a major counter offensive in their endless turf war with the black flies. Just think of it as a backwoods version of the Crips and the Bloods, where *you* supply the blood.

What is it about Mainers and black flies anyway? We certainly don't *love* them. Maybe we just love to complain about them? Then again, it's not exactly that either. It's more that other thing, that quirky Maine thing that is so much a part of the fabric of our Maine life.

I think of it as celebrating adversity. Not *di*-versity, mind you, although we've been known to do a fair amount of that as well. Nope, I'm talking about *ad*-versity. It seems that reveling in life's trials and tribulations is as quintessentially Maine as red hotdogs and whoopie pies with a Moxie chaser.

For Mainers, black flies share a category with ice storms, potholes, frost heaves, recessions (great or otherwise), mud season, and similar indignities that, to hear us tell it, would have crushed a lesser state years ago. We don't consider ourselves victims, though, not by a long shot. We're survivors!

Clearly, a well-developed sense of humor is the one absolutely indispensable tool in a Mainer's emergency survival kit. How else to explain The Maine Black Fly Breeders Association in Machias? I interviewed these folks once for CBS News *Sunday Morning* and found it darned near impossible to keep a straight face as various members, tongues firmly planted in cheeks, waxed eloquent about such creations as the Black Fly Swarm Dome.

In case you missed it, that's a Maine version of the glass snow globe you got for Christmas when you were a kid. Only when you shake this globe, instead of white flakes swirling around a church steeple, a swarm of black flies erupts in a dark menacing cloud and proceeds to swarm around a tiny Maine farmhouse. "Look kids. It's just like real life!"

Following the broadcast we got literally hundreds of responses, comments, and inquiries from folks across the country wanting to know where they could buy one. Now, don't you wish you'd thought of it?

In the summer of 1981, Marshall Dodge and I performed comedy shows in dozens of Maine towns, including one at Cumston Hall in Monmouth, where we invented something called "The Black Fly Festival." The theater was packed and the audience was having such a good time that they called us back for an encore. As we headed out onto the stage we had absolutely no idea what we'd do next.

Fortunately, the energy of the crowd supplemented by the adrenaline rush that always accompanies improvisational comedy (without a net) spurred us on and before long we had the crowd roaring as we listed the highlights of a festival that, according to us, was held annually in the IGA parking lot in Rangeley. Since the whole thing was an ad-lib, we were just making it up as we went along when we described the Miss Black Fly Competition as ". . . not just a beauty contest. Matter of fact, beauty don't hardly enter into it."

With a bit of polishing, that improvised routine soon became a staple of our act, eventually taking on a life of its own. There's a version of it on one of my early albums as well as in my book *Saturday Night at Moody's Diner*. It's even been published in a couple of anthologies.

Given the fact that Marshall and I fabricated the entire outlandish tale on the spur of the moment one long ago summer night, you can imagine my surprise when I stopped by a store in Presque Isle a few years back and spotted a poster advertising a Black Fly Festival that was being held somewhere in the area.

A bit of investigation revealed that this was by no means an isolated incident. Apparently life was indeed imitating art in a number of locations around the state.

I discovered, much to my chagrin, that several Black Fly Festivals have cropped up in Maine towns over the years and although I've never actually attended one, you never know, one of these days I just might.

If you do go, keep your eyes peeled. I won't be all that hard to spot. Just look for the tall guy with an extra large bottle of old time woodsman's fly dope in his back pocket wearing a "Celebrate Adversity!" T-shirt.

Moonlight in the Afternoon

Dark as a pocket? Dark as a cellar shelf? Whatever colorful term you choose, keeping a sunny disposition during early December in Maine can be a daunting proposition.

On the other hand, if it's not dark enough for you in tropical southern Maine, just gas up the car, head East by North East and motor on over to Washington County. My wife and I have been known do that for some "just us" time, before the final crescendo of holiday revelry hits.

Washington County, Maine, proudly bills itself as "The Sunrise County," not simply because it's a catchier slogan than "This Pharmacy No Longer Carries OxyContin," either. It's actually the easternmost hunk of real estate in entire nation, the first place the sun's rays strike U.S. soil.

The dark side is that it's also the first place that same sun sets again and this time of year, as we don our night vision goggles and grope our way toward the winter solstice, that mid-afternoon sunset can be a bit unnerving. At least it felt that way to me last time I drove east along "The Airline" in early December.

We were about thirty miles from the Canadian border headed due east when I crested a hill and was momentarily blinded by the glare of the full moon through the windshield. It was brighter than the high beams of the westbound semis. Full moon? High beams? A glance at the dashboard clock confirmed that it was pitch dark at 4:23 p.m. There's something seriously wrong with that.

We were headed to Calais for the annual downtown Friday night "Moonlight Madness" sale. Being easily seduced by the myriad details of small town life, it's the perfect event to jumpstart my holiday spirit. We arrived just as the big Christmas parade was forming and watched an impressive procession of lovingly decorated homemade floats departing from the staging area in the IGA parking lot. Santa himself was on hand, ho-ho-ho-ing enthusiastically from his perch high atop the Calais Fire Department's spit polished ladder truck, prompting a bit of speculation.

What if an emergency call came in during the parade and the fire engines had to rush off to fight a fire? We decided that since Santa was almost certainly on the fire department, he'd be thankful to find himself in the right place (no doubt with a chimney involved) at the right time.

Fortunately we managed to snag some wicked good holiday bargains while we were there. Although we somehow mustered the willpower to pass up the shocking pink hunting rifle (Barbie's first .22?) at 30% off in the gun case at the Calais True Value Hardware, we did fill our cart with several other treasures, including, but not limited to, three custom printed hoodies emblazoned with the following message printed in flashy Las Vegas style lettering, "Welcome to Fabulous Calais, Maine. What happens in Calais stays in Calais. . . . But nothing really happens in Calais."

Ah, but I beg to differ. Like me, my wife hails from a small town, (Marine on St. Croix, Minnesota, population 602 in the most recent census) and she, too, is a sucker for the little mom and pop shops that, despite the rising tide of chain stores, still exist on the Main streets of America. So we came, we saw, we did a little shopping by the silvery light of the afternoon moon.

At the local jewelry store a fresh faced teenager greeted us and handed my wife a card. "This is your 'gift list' card," he said. When she asked him how that worked he replied, "Oh, it's easy. You walk around the store and jot down all the things you like and then," nodding at me, "your husband will come in tomorrow and buy them for you." Brilliant! Now, that's what I call an economic stimulus plan!

We managed to have a terrific time, do our bit to prop up the perennially beleaguered Washington County economy, and get quite a bit of holiday shopping done all at the same time.

But, just in case my wife is reading this, I should mention that there *is* something special on my wish list this year. You know those "full spectrum" artificial daylight lamps? I hear they're perfect for staving off depression and boosting your energy during these long, dark December days. Who knows? If I had one of those lights I just might be able stay up and keep shopping until 8:30, heck maybe even 9 o'clock for next year's Moonlight Madness sale.

Ah . . . Mud Season

You know you've truly experienced a Maine winter when you start looking forward to mud season. By late March spring has already sprung for many folks elsewhere in the northeast. In Boston there might well be balmy breezes rustling through blossoming forsythia.

In Maine it's another story. About the time our neighbors to the west and south are tuning up their lawn mowers we're digging out our hip boots. It was ever thus and, in grand Maine tradition, which my mother calls "making a virtue of necessity," Mud Season has become a rite of passage and thus the subject of some of our most enduring "Maine stories." Here's a classic.

Having navigated fifty yards of knee-deep goop to reach the mail box at the end of his driveway, a nineteenth-century Maine farmer surveys the river of mud that constitutes the town road and notices a small, gray something moving slowly in his direction. A squirrel? Nope, too small for a squirrel, and a squirrel would move faster. Woodchuck? Wrong color. As it bobs slowly toward him he recognizes it as his neighbor's old fedora hat, apparently lost upstream.

Locating a fallen tree limb of sufficient length, he prepares to retrieve the drifting chapeau. Surely the road will be passable in a week or two. He'll return the hat to its owner then.

He deftly snags it, only to reveal his neighbor's bald pate and, beneath that, his upturned nose. "Kinda hard walkin', ain't it Harry?" says the farmer. "That it is!" replies his neighbor. "But it could be worse. At least I've still got my horse under me!"

When I was a young man living a mile or so down a dirt road, in Palmyra, I experienced a few "mud season moments" nearly as daunting.

The Raymond Road in those days was barely a road at all and the stretch between my house and Route 2 was virtually impassable for days at a time during mud season. When I say impassable I mean *nobody* got through! Not the mail, ambulance, or police. I suppose that if our house had caught fire during mud season we'd have had to fight the flames with a garden hose until the road dried up.

During one particularly nasty stretch of isolation, virtually marooned for days in a sea of mud, my patience finally ran out. It hadn't rained for a day or two and the sun was out. Why not give it a try? Why not indeed!

I cranked the engine to life and in two minutes I'd managed to hopelessly mire the rear wheels of my old Dodge D-100 pick-up without even leaving my driveway! Abandoning the truck and donning my high-water boots I trudged the half-mile or so up the road to the farmhouse next door. Fortunately, my neighbor "Fod" Sprague was home and willing to come to my aid. Always even tempered and practical, Fod started up his ancient and indestructible Land Rover (with it's sturdy bumper winch) and we headed back into the fray.

I was confident that Fod's rig would have me out and on the road in a jiffy. Hooking the winch to my front bumper, he gave me a thumbs up. What followed was a half hour or so of screaming engines, groaning metal, and flying mud. When the racket subsided the air was thick with blue exhaust fumes and both vehicles sat motionless, axle deep in mud. Stepping out from behind the wheel, Fod flashed me a gap-toothed grin. I felt like an idiot. But clearly he was just starting to enjoy himself.

Pausing to light an unfiltered Camel, he chortled, "More'n one way to skin a cat," and motioned for me to follow him back to the farmhouse for the heavy artillery, his massive John Deere tractor.

An hour or so later, having succeeded in extricating both trucks, we parked them side by side on a patch of high ground behind my woodshed, and that's exactly where they stayed for the week or so it took for mud season to loosen its gooey grip on the Raymond Road.

Maybe the reason we Mainers tend to canonize our mud season stories is that they serve as an important annual reminder that sometimes, when things are really difficult, the very best thing we can do, in fact the *only* thing we can do, is sit back and wait for the situation to improve on its own, and somehow, amazingly, it always seems to do just that.

A Rafter Snapper

Mainers of a certain vintage will take comfort in the knowledge that the traditional January Thaw usually arrives right on schedule. It's amazing what just two or three days of bright sun and daytime temps in the fifties can do to boost our spirits. Of course the fact that we call it a thaw in the first place pretty much guarantees that it will come with a freeze on either end.

Actually, this year's pre-thaw freeze wasn't too bad, with daytime temps in the teens and twenties and a little snow every now and then, it was just typical Maine winter weather.

But the post-thaw freeze has been a whole other kettle of frozen smelts. At this writing, the Montreal Express, which arrived a week ago, is still hanging around. A friend in Aroostook County recently reported temps in the mid-twenties, which sounds fine until you realize that the mid-twenties she's talking about have a minus sign in front of 'em. Add a stiff breeze and the wind chill will knock it down another fifteen or twenty degrees. Those are the kind of numbers that make you to think twice before making a trip to the privy.

Mind (and body) numbing cold weather is of course a cherished part of Maine folklore. When I was a kid the old timers called long, sub-zero nights "rafter snappers," a phrase I never understood until I moved inland to a little cabin surrounded by acres of tall trees.

One night, during a particularly frigid cold snap, I was awakened in the wee hours by what sounded like rifle shots echoing through the woods around the cabin. My first groggy thought was that it was a darned cold night for folks to be out jacking deer.

When I mentioned the shooting spree to old John down at the El Hill Store the next morning, he explained that the "shots" I'd heard probably weren't gunshots at all, but the sound of trees exploding! He went on to explain that when it gets cold enough, the moist sap in the tree trunks freezes solid, eventually expanding to the point where the trunk literally explodes. The same phenomenon occurs in the beams and rafters of unheated barns and outbuildings, hence the term "rafter snapper."

Back then I managed to heat my little cabin entirely with wood, using a cast iron 24-inch box stove capable of cranking out plenty of BTUs. But even fully loaded with seasoned rock maple, the two-foot firebox was simply too small to hold a fire for more than six or seven hours. That meant that somebody (I'll give you three guesses and the first two don't count) had to stoke the stove every few hours or the fire would die out. With no backup heat source, that was something you'd want to avoid if at all possible.

My system worked OK until a sudden-onset white-out blizzard forced an unscheduled overnight stay in Camden. Upon my return the next morning I found all the canned goods on the pantry shelf and even the milk in the refrigerator frozen solid!

Of course any stretch of super cold weather is bound to give rise to a fresh crop of "how cold was it" stories. Most Mainers of my generation have heard tales of the big freeze of 1911, or was it 1913? Either way, folks living in Boothbay Harbor back then tell of ice so thick in the inner harbor that fishing boats were literally frozen in their berths, and there are still some old black and white photos around showing Model Ts parked on the ice a stone's throw from Tumbler Island! I remember sometime in the late 50s hiking across the mud flats at low tide on great mushy cakes of frozen seawater.

So, how cold was it this time around? Well, I did hear on the local news that the drawbridge between Kittery and Portsmouth had frozen in the open position, forcing traffic to be re-routed for a day or so. That'll get your attention.

But, my favorite story involved a road grader operator in some northern Vermont town who stopped at a local convenience store for a cup of hot coffee. After climbing back in the cab with the steaming cup, he changed his mind, went back into the store, and picked up a couple of jelly donuts. He purchased the donuts, chatted with the clerk for a few minutes and left. Returning to the grader, he picked up his cup to take a sip and discovered that, in the short time he'd been gone, his piping hot coffee had frozen solid!

Winter Wonderland

Gazing out at the pristine snow-covered landscape just beyond my living room window I'm momentarily overwhelmed by the realization that I live in a winter wonderland. The key phrase in the preceding sentence is "gazing out at . . ." which clearly indicates that I'm observing the phenomenon from a safe distance. Also, please note that in this context my use of the term "wonderland" is meant to connote incredulity rather than awe, as in "I *wonder* why the heck I'm not tanning on a beach in Florida right now!"

To say that winter is not my favorite time of year in Maine is an understatement. The almost complete lack of sunlight would be depressing enough without precipitously plunging temperatures accompanied by 50-mph arctic blasts capable of flash freezing human flesh in a matter of seconds. Think I'm exaggerating? The weatherman is predicting a wind chill factor of -30 degrees today. So I guess that means if you slip on the ice while attempting to retrieve the morning paper in your bathrobe and slippers you've got like five minutes to live? Thanks for the heads up.

Let's face it. Wintertime in Maine is a lot like camping out for several months in a walk-in freezer, occasionally venturing forth to skate along highways and back roads coated with "wintery mix," creating the sort of treacherous road conditions that tow truck drivers must fantasize about all summer long.

"But Tim," you're probably thinking, "you're a Mainer. Aren't you supposed to love the Maine winters?" Whoever sold you that line of baloney is probably from away.

I experienced my first Maine winter over a half century ago when they were far more severe than the ones we've come to expect in the era of global warming, and frankly I don't ever recall much discussion about folks "enjoying" a Maine winter. A lively chat around the old woodstove back then would most likely have involved swapping coping strategies for surviving until mud season without going completely round the bend.

Of course, it's quite possible that my distaste for winter developed at least partly in response to being tossed in at the deep end of the snow bank as it were. I was, after all, born in Northern Aroostook County, just a stone's throw from the Canadian border. "The County" has long been famous for its severe winter weather. If you doubt that, you have a standing invitation to attend my next mid-winter performance at The Caribou Performing Arts Center. When you arrive and pull into the parking lot please note that more than half your fellow audience members are driving snowmobiles.

Although I don't have many specific memories of those harsh Aroostook winters in my early childhood, I've seen enough photos to give me a pretty good idea of what it was like. One of my favorites from the old family album is a black and white photo of my mom bundled up in a wool coat, muffler, hat, and gloves, clearly hovering on the brink of hypothermia yet somehow managing to look stylish as she pushes my brother and me along a snowy sidewalk in Limestone, Maine, circa 1953.

We're just a couple of toddlers swaddled in puffy snowsuits squinting out at the frigid landscape, but the part of the photo that always draws my eye is a small dark cross shaped object that appears to be floating in a sea of white several feet above my mother's head.

At first glance this shape might conjure up notions of some otherworldly spiritual apparition or even one of those blurry snapshots of an indistinct object that's either an interplanetary U.F.O. or a hastily tossed hubcap. Upon closer inspection it becomes clear that the dark cross in the photo is, in fact, the upper third of an old wooden telephone pole.

The confusion comes from the fact that the first twelve or fourteen feet of the pole are completely obscured by a white snowdrift. That's right chummy. The pile of snow lining the the road is taller than the roof of your trailer!

So, I guess that brings us back to where we started. If I'm so darned sick of Maine winters why do I stay here instead of heading for Florida like so many other snowbirds? I don't honestly know. I suppose I'm just used to it after all this time. Maybe if I didn't have the winter to complain about I wouldn't know what to do with myself. Of course there's an old Maine saying that explains it as well as anything else: "If you can't take the winters, you don't deserve the summers!"

Oh! Deer!

Where does the time go? It seems like just the other day we were marking winter's end with the arrival of all the traditional harbingers of a Maine spring—potholes, frost heaves, mud, and black flies. Now, suddenly, deer season is upon us. If you're a recent transplant you might want to get a pad of paper and take notes because whatever you think deer season is going to be, whatever it may have been in your previous life "back home," the Maine version is going to serve up a whole 'nother cup of venison stew altogether.

Although the dates differ slightly for folks who prefer to stalk these woodland creatures with more arcane weaponry such as crossbows and muzzle loaders (we'll be dealing with Buicks in due course), traditional Maine hunters tend to don their camo and blaze orange uniforms at Halloween and rarely find it necessary to change until it's time to sit down for Thanksgiving dinner.

"What," you may ask, "does any of this have to do with me? I'm not even a hunter." Well, depending on your location, even if you aren't a hunter, deer season is going to have a significant impact on your life.

For example, in large swaths of rural Washington, Aroostook, Hancock, Penobscot, and a few other Maine counties, commercial life during deer season slows to a trickle, occasionally grinding to a complete halt. Want to get your dock taken out before the lake freezes? That's not going to happen during hunting season. The same holds for many other non-essentials like haircuts, valve jobs, painting, wall papering, ditch digging . . . the list goes on. Even the local volunteer fire department is likely to have fewer boots on the ground. Don't misunderstand me. They won't let your trailer burn down. But, if your cat gets stuck up a tree you're not going to get her back until after deer season.

On the other hand, business at local mom and pop convenience stores will be booming since they stock all the basic necessities of a successful hunt—beef jerky, chewing tobacco, pickled eggs, ammo, camo, and Bud Lite. My favorite Maine General Store, Princeton Variety on Route 1, also sells what I consider to be the perfect T-shirt for deer season in Maine. It's blaze orange (of course) with A.T.F. printed in big, bold letters across the front. Underneath there's a line of smaller print that reads "Alcohol, Tobacco and Firearms. Sounds like my kind of convenience store!"

Of course not all hunters are successful in their quest to bag the elusive white tail. Although they come here looking for deer, a fairly high percentage of out-of-state hunters end up mostly finding beer. Still, if you know where to look (and you didn't hear this from me) there are other ways to take home a trophy buck even if you haven't seen a deer all week. Here's how it works.

On Saturday nights certain of our local nimrods have been known to frequent the "beer store," just sitting around swapping stories until a party of unsuccessful "outta state" hunters stops in for a case of beer or three before heading home in disgrace. A conversation is struck up, in the course of which certain key questions are posed by the natives. Questions like:

"If you was to shoot a deer what type would you aim for? A buck? What size? How many points?" You get the idea.

Following this little fireside chat, punctuated by a few well timed winks and nods and a bit of idle speculation along the lines of, "How much a nice deer like that would be worth to a feller heading back home to show it off to his friends and family" the natives exit with the not-too-subtle parting suggestion that the "sports" might find it well worth their while to stop by the store again the next morning before heading home.

Mainers of a certain independent, practical-minded bent, having already acquired enough of "The Governor's Beef" to last through 'til spring, have often found this annual ritual to be an excellent source of cash to supplement the family income during the long winter ahead.

Oh yeah, one more thing. You know that Buick I mentioned earlier? Well, as it happens, some of our more enterprising citizens have devised a method of stocking the family freezer simply by utilizing a skill set honed in dozens of demolition derbies at county fairs around the state.

This technique, properly executed, has enabled more than one Ricky Craven wannabe to bag that trophy buck without so much as firing a single shot.

Cabin Fever Reliever

Step right up! What's your pleasure: marathon cribbage tournaments, the NFL playoffs on a large screen TV? Maybe it's finally time to tackle that ship-in-a-bottle project you've been talking about for the last five winters. The details don't matter all that much as long as you can find an activity sufficiently absorbing to fill the dull winter days and stave off the more debilitating effects of "cabin fever."

One of my personal "cabin fever reliever" strategies involves indulging in a few hours of harmless motorcycle fantasy. When the wind is howling and the snow is halfway up the kitchen window, all it takes is a hot mug of coffee, a few of my favorite motorcycle magazines, and my big leather recliner and within minutes I've got the motor running and I'm outta here.

I was introduced to the quixotic joys of motorcycling at the tender age of fifteen, when I was offered a ride on a friend's little Czechoslovakian built Jawa dirt bike. At 50ccs, it wasn't what most folks would consider a proper motorcycle, and that first ride amounted to approximately 38 highly exhilarating seconds careening across a lumpy cow meadow on Bailey Island on a warm midsummer night. I didn't care that I looked ridiculous and had no idea what I was doing. I was smitten. Whatever it was that I'd just experienced I wanted to do it again and again. That was in the summer of 1966 and I've been riding motorcycles ever since.

These days if you mention that you're a motorcyclist folks will inevitably ask, "You got a Harley?" Nope, never did, probably never will. When my love affair with motorcycles began, the iconic American brand Harley-Davidson had fallen on hard times, driven to the brink of bankruptcy by more reliable, less expensive, more technologically sophisticated machines from companies with odd sounding names like Honda, Suzuki, and Yamaha.

My very first bike, acquired at age eighteen, was a Honda Sport 65, red with a chrome gas tank, a faux leopard skin seat cover, and a playboy bunny sticker on the side cover, all of which somehow translated to "cool" in my adolescent brain. I bought it for $150 from a used car sales-man in Lewiston. Come to think of it, that explains a lot.

It was fun while it lasted, which unfortunately wasn't very long. A popular advertising jingle back then promised that you'd "meet the nic-est people on a Honda." Well, within a month of owning mine I'd man-aged to "meet," and subsequently get run over by, an elderly lady in a massive battleship gray Plymouth Fury.

She may very well have been a nice person but the experience certain-ly wasn't. I'll spare you the gory details except to say that it was a bizarre, low speed encounter, which I survived with only a broken leg and a lifelong commitment to defensive riding. Thankfully, in the forty-plus years since that little dust up, I've ridden over 100,000 miles without further injury.

In that time I've owned about a dozen bikes: two-strokes, four-strokes, and no-strokes, beaters and showroom-new models ranging from 350 to 1100 ccs with 1,2,3,4 and "no" cylinders. In case you're won-dering about the "no-stroke, no cylinder" model, that one was a metal-flake orange 1975 Suzuki RE-5 Rotary, the world's only mass-produced rotary engine motorcycle, which actually *was* pretty cool!

My first big motorcycle, bought second hand from a friend in 1973 for $500, was a Suzuki T-500 Titan. Of course, that's not big by today's stan-dards, but back in the day it was a well-regarded road machine with respectable power, a top speed approaching triple digits and the ability to cruise all day at 60–70 mph in relative comfort, with the accent on relative.

Hey, you want comfort? I know where you can find a gray 1964 Ply-mouth previously driven by a little old lady. It's in great condition except for a large leg-shaped dent in the front bumper.

In the spring of 1974, I took the Suzuki on my first long motorcycle road trip, a three-week 4000-mile odyssey that included a rush-hour breakdown on the Woodrow Wilson Bridge in Washington, D.C., a torna-do in the aptly named town of Blowing Rock, N.C., and twelve water-logged hours on rain slick roads in Tennessee.

That trip might well have persuaded some other neophyte biker to seriously consider taking up golf. Not me. My reaction was the same as it had been after my debut ride in the cow meadow. I just couldn't wait to do it again! Hmmm, now there's an idea.

My Coat Rack

Now, where did I put my list of New Year's resolutions? Oh yeah, now I remember, I didn't make a list this year. Come to think of it I didn't make one last year, either. Hmmm, when did this revolutionary trend begin?

Let's face it. Opting out of the time-honored practice of annual New Year's resolutions is a bit radical given the fact that listing everything we plan to do differently in the coming year is as American as apple pie, ice cream, eggnog, turkey, another slice of apple pie, please, gravy, mashed potatoes, Twinkies, fad diets, self-help seminars, Nordic Tracks, gym memberships, six-pack abs, the nicotine patch, and thirty-day rehabs.

I'm pretty sure my previous commitment to annual lifestyle make-overs began to unravel during my last really big everything-must-go family yard sale. Maybe it had something to do with schlepping my barely used exercise equipment from a dusty corner of the basement into the brilliant sunshine on our front lawn. I was huffing and puffing at a fairly alarming rate by the time I got it up the stairs and, as I paused to catch my breath, it dawned on me that the past half hour or so was probably the most vigorous workout I would ever experience with my rather expensive experiment in self-improvement.

The fact that my wife, a lifelong fitness buff herself, had taken to referring to it as "your coatrack" should have been a tip off.

The seeds of rebellion planted that spring morning soon began to sprout and grow. I realized that, despite decades of resolutions, made with varying decrees of resolve, I had almost never (scratch that) I had *never* actually succeeded in bringing about any of the desired lifestyle changes using this approach.

In fact, to be perfectly honest about it (and if you're not being honest about something like this you're basically cheating at solitaire) instead of stimulating positive change, all those lists of well meaning resolutions sooner or later (mostly sooner) ended up as abandoned projects. Ultimately this left me feeling more like a failure than if I'd never made the darned lists in the first place.

By now I'm sure you're thinking that I'm just some old sourpuss, devoid of optimism and hope and resigned to a life of bad attitudes and even worse personal habits.

Ah, but you're wrong! In fact, since I decided to forego those unrealistic, setting-myself-up-for-defeat annual lists, my *actual* tally of genuine positive lifestyle improvements has continued to get longer.

An excellent example of this improved self-improvement record is that I'm currently more than halfway through my fourth consecutive year as a non-smoker. I've lost count of the number of times I firmly resolved to give up cigarettes on New Year's day, only to find myself guiltily torching a cheroot, like some schoolboy out behind the barn, a day, a month, or a year later and feeling that much worse about myself for having failed yet again.

"So," you may be wondering, "if the New Year's resolutions didn't work, what did?" Simple, that age-old motivator of human progress, enlightened self-interest. I realized that setting some arbitrary start date was doomed to failure for the same reason that enlightened self-interest is most likely to succeed: in a word, *motivation!*

Ever since Oog and Og quit bickering over their dwindling supply of boiled palm fronds and decided to pool their resources on a mastodon hunt, enlightened self-interest has been the prime motivator of genuine human progress.

As long as I was trying to quit smoking for some abstract reason like the advent of a new year it wasn't going to happen. Nor was I likely to be swayed by the comments of well-meaning doctors, nurses, friends, and family members. The fact that they were motivated didn't mean I was. I'd need to be prodded into action by personal experience if I was ever going to change.

As I write this, the White House and the U.S. Congress are still arm wrestling at the edge of the fiscal cliff. I have no idea whether they will be successful. What I do know is that if they do succeed, you can thank the cliff itself. Why? Because avoiding a catastrophic economic meltdown is a powerful motivator.

In the case of my cigarette habit, motivation arrived via $5.00-a-pack pricing, a fiscal pothole hopefully deep enough to get me off tobacco road for good.

These days I'm more likely to make a "gratitude list" than any New Year's resolutions. If you're wondering how my exercise routine is going, um, check back with me on that next year.

A Holly Dazed Shopping Guide

Well, it's here again, the week before Christmas, that magical time when I finally sit down with a glass of chilled eggnog and start to get serious about my holiday gift list. I know, I know, a lot of you are laboring under the delusion that your Christmas shopping should be all finished by now. But where's the fun in that?

Aren't people constantly carping about how the Christmas season comes earlier and earlier each year? It certainly seems that way. Yet folks continue to work themselves into a premature, artificial, and totally pointless early shopping frenzy in response to a bunch of blatant marketing gimmicks like Black Friday and Cyber Monday.

As far as I'm concerned, real men do their Christmas shopping, all of it, at the last possible second.

Over the years I've noticed that women generally employ a completely different strategy, characterized by a kind of low-level holiday gift foraging throughout the year. Whether pawing over boxes of costume jewelry at a spring yard sale, queuing up for a Christmas-in-July fundraiser at the Methodist Church, or wandering around an autumn craft fair, they're always on the lookout for that just-right gift for Great Aunt Matilda. This approach seems to be based on the quaint notion that once all the shopping and wrapping are out of the way, they'll be able to relax and enjoy the season.

But, as any man who's being honest about it can tell you, nothing matches the sheer adrenaline/testosterone rush we get from charging (fiscally as well as physically) down the aisles of our local WalMart, Rite Aid, and Home Depot on Christmas Eve, competing for the few remaining items everybody else has managed to ignore completely since Halloween. It's a heady thing, an impulse buyer's dream.

And really, when are you ever going to see bargains like this again? I'm sure mom will just love that Makita 18V lithium ion, cordless 14-piece combo hedge trimmer, drill press, and die-tapping kit at 65% off! Well, OK, maybe not, but it's the last display model on the shelf so that's what she's getting.

See what I mean? No soul searching, no comparison-shopping, no mulling it over and consulting consumer reports. I'm talking about power shopping Marvel Comics style. Bang! Pow! Zap! We're outta there.

One really big advantage to be gained from this shopping technique is that you'll never have to worry about getting your friends and family members the same thing somebody else already gave them. Trust me, if it's still on the shelf at midnight on Christmas Eve you can safely assume that nobody else is giving one to anybody!

But just in case my non-male-bonding-eligible readers are starting to feel a little left out here, buck up ladies. Be of good cheer! There's one other gift-giving alternative absolutely guaranteed to produce the same high degree of exclusivity at a bargain basement price. You guessed it! When it comes to one-of-a-kind gifts you can't beat homemade, and the best part is anybody can do it!

I remember one early childhood Christmas when two of my siblings and I, each under the age of ten, discovered knitting at the very same time. I'm not sure how that got started. But, once it did we were unstoppable. Like sweatshop workers in a Dickens novel, toiling relentlessly from sunup to sundown, we eventually produced impressive piles of misshapen potholders, perfect Christmas gifts for friends and relatives alike.

Being the artistic one (a.k.a. the one who doesn't follow directions well), I quickly discovered that if you don't stop knitting when all four sides of your work are more or less of equal length, your potholder will begin to magically transform itself into something completely different. What that would turn out to be exactly was always subject to interpretation.

For instance, if mine ever reached more than a foot and a half in length I called it a scarf. If it exhibited a tendency to get wider and narrower as it curved and dipped into abstract shapes it was christened a wall hanging.

Whatever its final form, you can bet that no one who received one of my youthful masterpieces that year was in the slightest danger of stumbling upon its doppelganger under the Christmas tree, in this or any other life.

Whatever technique you employ, however, always remember, it's not the gift, it's the thought that counts. If you doubt the veracity of that sentiment, simply wait until next spring and visit those yard sales I mentioned earlier, at which you're sure to find plenty of re-gifting opportunities, one of which may even be just right for Aunt Matilda.

IV

Life is a Road Trip

How My Dad Invented the S.U.V.

Next time you're cruising around the highways and byways of America take a break from text messaging and latte slurping and spend a few minutes observing the traffic around you. Depending on where you happen to be, between 40 and 70 percent of the vehicles sharing the road with you will be sport utility vehicles, or S.U.V.s for short.

To qualify in this category a vehicle must meet a few basic qualifications. Four doors and a hatch? Check. Power to all four wheels? Check. High ride height? Check. Big gas guzzling engine? Um, well, maybe. There's a growing category of "Cute Utes" like the Honda CRV and Toyota Rav4 with smaller, more fuel efficient engines. But the original big gas guzzling variety (think Chevy Suburban, Ford Expedition, and Jeep Grand Cherokee) is still alive and well.

So how did something that didn't even exist fifty years ago come to dominate the American road, and who came up with the idea anyway? I can't answer the first part. But the second part is easy. My dad invented it.

Ah, you scoff! But I swear on a stack of old Hemmings Motor News it's true. I saw it with my own eyes. It all started on a late fall afternoon back in the early 1960s, when my dad brought home an ancient Willys Overland station wagon that had obviously seen better days. The Willys was a tall four-door, four-wheel-drive station wagon type rig built in the 40s and 50s by the same folks who built the iconic Jeep our GIs drove through WWII. It even looked like a Jeep, only taller and you could ride in it without getting rained on. Like its spunky little military forebear, however, the Willys was no speed demon. Its tiny four-cylinder engine would move it from 0 to 60 mph in about, hmmm, well, come to think of it 60 mph is awfully fast. How about 53 mph later this afternoon when the breeze picks up?

My dad had a habit of acquiring such vehicles as his winter projects, and I could tell it would take plenty of long cold nights to whip that particular rolling pile of junk into anything I'd want to be seen in next summer.

So, I'd pretty much forgotten about it by the time the ice was out. Then, I came home from school one afternoon and noticed the garage doors flung open revealing a beautiful, shiny, pea-green vehicle that I didn't even recognize. As my dad backed it into our driveway I couldn't help but notice the deep burbling sound emanating from the spiffy new twin chromed exhaust pipes. Hmmm, what have we here?

What we had is what I've come to think of as America's first S.U.V. Over the winter my dad had managed to transform that tired, rusty old Willys into a new sort of 4 X 4. I'd never seen anything like it and neither had anybody else. Gone was the sputtering four-cylinder engine, replaced by a seriously powerful Ford V8. Big wheels with brand new off-road tires put the power to the ground through a beefed up truck transmission. The fender chrome glistened in the sun. The fresh bodywork and shiny paint made it look brand new.

A few weeks later the whole family packed into the Willys for her maiden voyage to our camp in northern Maine, and when I say "packed in," I'm not kidding. There was mom, dad, our big old dog, three kids, and a week's worth of gear occupying every inch of available space. What didn't fit inside was lashed onto the roof or packed into the eighteen-foot Grumman canoe (with trolling motor attached) we were hauling on a trailer behind us. It must have presented quite a sight to the Maine State Trooper who pulled us over as we were climbing a particularly steep hill north of Skowhegan at a speed north of 85 mph!

His blue light went on, we pulled over, and the officer walked up to the open driver's side window. I'll never forget what happened next. The officer stood for several long moments slowly rotating his head from the hood of the Willys to the family inside to the overloaded roof rack to the boat trailer and back again several times. Finally, he spoke and his voice was almost reverent. "Sir," he said staring slack-jawed at my dad, "I'm not going to give you a ticket because nobody would believe me anyway. But, I am going to ask you to get out and open the hood so I can see what the (bleep bleep) you have under there!"

The Perfect Summer Job

When I was fifteen I got the perfect summer job. The fact that it involved driving cars should surprise no one. Having had the good fortune to enter my teens just as America was hitting the crest of its love affair with the automobile and given my prolonged exposure to near-toxic levels of chromium, futuristic design excesses, and jet propelled marketing hype, I really had no choice other than to become a car guy.

That summer I was a couple of years shy of the minimum age to obtain a Maine driver's permit, a fact that did nothing to dampen my automotive ardor. Like the fictional Mr. Toad, I was consumed by one devilishly simple goal: to get behind the wheel of a car, any car, as soon and as often as humanly possible.

Back then, my dad owned a shipyard and in hopes of instilling a healthy work ethic pretty much required me to spend a portion of my school vacation punching a time clock in the family business. Fortunately, my job description didn't require any particular mechanical aptitude beyond the skills needed to scrub the restrooms, sweep the docks, and bail out the occasional skiff.

Looking back I can see that my dad was motivated by a sincere belief that a few hours of hard work each day would go a long way toward offsetting the natural tendency of adolescent boys to get into mischief. Although he meant well, he couldn't possibly have known that the shipyard job itself would end up providing me with a golden opportunity to fulfill my dream of joining the ranks of Maine's unlicensed drivers.

In those innocent pre-E.P.A. days, pretty much all of the considerable garbage generated each week at the shipyard was indiscriminately tossed into 55-gallon drums. When they were full it was time to make a "dump run," which involved loading all the trash barrels into the bed of a battered old pickup truck and hauling them off to the town dump. Since dump runs required approximately the same skill set as dock sweeping and toilet cleaning, I almost always got to participate.

While riding shotgun in the truck's cab one sunny afternoon it dawned on me that I was exactly where I had been longing to be, in a vehicle, only a couple of feet from the steering wheel, one small ignition key-turn from being the driver. How hard could it be to cajole a coworker into letting me take a turn behind the wheel, just for fun?

Not hard at all, as it turned out. Since the dump run didn't require highly trained workers, most of the drivers were new guys barely out of their teens themselves and it didn't take a whole lot of convincing to get them to go along with some harmless hijinks.

So, if you happened to be walking along Townsend Avenue that particular summer and you noticed an overloaded pickup truck proceeding somewhat erratically toward Boothbay Center driven by one highly excited fifteen-year-old boy, well, that would have been me.

How I avoided running into (literally or figuratively) the local constabulary, or worse yet, some innocent tourist from Duluth, remains a mystery. Nevertheless I managed to make several such drives without incident. Needless to say, these brief road trips to the dump only served to increase my behind-the-wheel confidence, thereby whetting my appetite for more of the same.

Which brings me to that perfect summer job. My friend Luigi, a little older and, if it were possible, even more car crazy than I, not only had a driver's license, he had his own car! He also had a summer job charging tourists a buck an hour to let him park their shiny new Ford Galaxies and Chevy Impalas in his uncle's vacant lot. In just a few weeks he'd already taken in several hundred dollars. So, when he offered me 50% of the daily cash income simply for the privilege of running the operation on weekends while he took in the drag races at Beech Ridge Speedway, I jumped at the chance.

I was actually going to get paid to drive other people's cars! It was the perfect summer job. At least that's what I thought until someone pointed out that Luigi had the *real* perfect summer job.

"Whaddaya mean?" I protested, "He's not even working this weekend. He's off at the drag races."

Which was, of course, the point. Luigi spent every weekend that summer sipping cold sodas and watching drag races while collecting half the money I earned working at his uncle's parking lot—and that, my friends, is the perfect summer job!

Life in the Slow Lane

The late Charles Kuralt, a frequent visitor to the Boothbay region, once referred to Maine as a place where it's possible to become so relaxed that your self-winding watch stops working. Aside from the fact that any reference to self-winding watches these days is likely to draw a blank stare, it's easy to see what he meant.

Many generations of summer folks have, in fact, trekked to Maine to do exactly this sort of unwinding. The old timers even have a name for them. Seasonal visitors seeking relief from life in the fast lane were traditionally referred to as "rusticators." According to my dictionary, to rusticate is to "go to, live in, or spend time in the country," and in case you haven't glanced up from your iPhone recently, you may have forgotten that most of Maine still qualifies as "the country."

I was actually thinking about rusticators the other day while idling in a line of traffic waiting for the gal in the lime green vest to rotate her official traffic paddle from "stop" to "slow" and wave me on through a four-block section of Portland's Washington Avenue currently undergoing refurbishment. I never mind a few extra minutes of drive time in my old roadster. With the top down, the sun on my face, and the aroma of warm asphalt in my nostrils, my thoughts naturally drifted toward the topic of summer traffic.

My ruminations no doubt sprung from the fact that I'm a sucker for irony. And there's plenty of irony in any story featuring throngs of urban escapees jammed into the family Prius, heading north in search of inner tranquility, only to discover just beyond the Welcome to Maine sign several cement barricades flanked by flashing yellow lights with digital messages advising: "Caution! Road Construction Ahead, Next Four Months!"

Welcome to Maine—Life in the Slow Lane.

It's no great secret that Maine's highways are always being repaired at the most inconvenient time, right in the middle of tourist season. What? You thought maybe we'd be doing this in January?

No, the real head scratcher is that with mile after mile of Route 1, plus dozens of other roads from Kittery to Fort Kent, under construction, legions of Maine-bound, hypertensive serenity-seekers paradoxically find themselves stuck in a situation where there's no rational alternative *other than* to relax . . . though they rarely figure that out until they've exhausted all other options.

Even those of us with native status, who've been to this dance often enough to know better, occasionally succumb to the urge to pass some lurching, lumbering motorhome with out-of-state plates only to find ourselves an hour and a half later just a couple of car lengths and maybe three seconds ahead of that same vehicle when we finally pull off Route 1 into the Moody's Diner parking lot.

Native or neophyte, we all eventually arrive at the same conclusion— no amount of horn honking, hollering, or digit waving is going to push this particular river along any more quickly than it's inclined to move anyway.

The good news, grasshopper, is that once you've accepted this Zenlike worldview the other views you encounter along Maine's scenic roads might inspire some surprising insights. Let's face it, when forward motion is in the 10- to 15-mph range you have a lot more time to notice details than you would rushing along the same stretch of blacktop at 55 or 60, which leads to such observations as:

"Hey honey, have you ever noticed that none of those worm diggers out on the clam flats in Cod Cove seem to be wearing a belt?"

And let's not forget the road crew workers themselves. With their picks, shovels, pneumatic jack hammers, and massive earth moving equipment they put on quite a show all by themselves. I was reminded of this a few years back when my wife and I visited England and took in an exhibit of rare antiquities at the Victoria and Albert Museum in London.

The show featured a once-in-a-lifetime opportunity to view the actual personal sketchbooks of iconic renaissance visionary Leonardo da Vinci. One sketch in particular caught my eye. It was a drawing of several workmen repairing a section of a fifteenth-century Florentine piazza. Something about the scene seemed eerily familiar but it took me a while to figure out exactly what it was. Then it hit me! Leonardo had drawn five laborers, each holding a shovel. But only one of them was actually working. The others were leaning intently on their own shovels and watching that first man dig a hole. Just like out on Route 1!

Roadster Redux

As a fan of the British documentary film series *UP!*, I'm inclined to accept the basic premise of the quote, "Give me the child until age seven and I will give you the man," on which the films are based. The origin of the line may be obscure. But, the case for its veracity strikes me as pretty solid.

Maybe that's why I love convertibles. There's certainly no denying that long before I hit the seven-year mark, I'd accumulated enough first hand experience with these magical metal chariots to leave a permanent imprint on my all-too-malleable young brain.

Although I'll probably never know what, if any, developmental mischief was percolating in my noggin back in those halcyon days, the fact remains that I'm a sucker for a ragtop. Not just any ragtop, either, mind you.

Fortunately, early childhood exposed me to a fine selection of genuine classics from another British Invasion immediately preceding the musical one led by The Beatles, The Rolling Stones, et al. Come to think of it, the one I'm referring too also featured a talented, entertaining lineup of charismatic Brits.

They came in the years following the end of World War Two with names like Jaguar, Triumph, and MG emblazoned in chrome script across their fenders. Upon arrival they proceeded to attack America's winding back roads with a vengeance, preaching the gospel of "motoring," a brand new form of four-wheeled outdoor summer sport.

The typically quirky Brit term for a cloth-topped sports car of this era is "drop head coupe," a colorful phrase that never caught on with Americans. On this side of the pond we called these tiny topless two-seaters "roadsters," and when I was barely old enough to walk across town alone and shoot aggies on the school playground, my older sisters were zipping around in some of the sharpest examples on the planet, including such automotive icons as the 1953 MG TD and the sensuous XK120 Jaguar.

I was only six when my sister Liza gave me my first ride in her diminutive MG roadster. Actually, given that car's cramped interior, my youth provided an ergonomic advantage in that I could slide into the cockpit without folding myself up like a jackknife.

That first ride was pure magic. I'd just settled into the leather-clad bucket seat (it really did resemble a bucket with the front lopped off) and was admiring the genuine wood dash with its simple, purposeful array of gauges, when my sister fired up the engine.

The sound proceeding from beneath the "bonnet" and rippling across the warm summer evening was glorious. The Brits have a word (of course) for that sound too. The symphony generated by a proper British roadster is always "rorty," which my *New Oxford American Dictionary* defines as "Boisterous and high spirited." Actually, that pretty much describes the whole magical experience of my first roadster ride.

Have you ever had a dream of flying? It was like that only more so. The symphonic blend of mechanical sounds, the warm breeze swirling around us, the blur of passing scenery, the intoxicating olfactory cocktail of pine trees, salt sea air, sun-warmed leather, and partially burned hydrocarbons. I was hooked!

Though I was well into my fifth decade when I finally got a ragtop of my own, it was worth the wait. Though not a Brit, "Zelda," our 1986 Mercedes 560 SL, *is* the car J.R. Ewing drives in the opening sequence of "Dallas." In fact when any 80s era movie or TV show needed to suggest money and class, they simply ordered up a Mercedes SL.

The fact that she's 27 years old, with 160K-plus miles on the clock, a nice patina of dings and a *Blue Book* value somewhere south of a used Hyundai does nothing to diminish her timeless appeal.

I recently took Zelda out of storage for our traditional spring shakedown cruise. Following a trip to the local carwash, we burbled through the take-out window at Starbucks and collected the usual chorus of oohs and ahhhs from the hoi polloi.

The smiles and waves continued as we motored along attending to mundane weekday tasks. As I prepared to leave the dry cleaner's, a harried young mom exited her kiddie-seat and Black Lab equipped Volvo station wagon, paused, smiled, and said, "Nice car."

"Yup," I nodded. "And the cheapest form of therapy known to man." Responding to her blank stare, I explained, "You see, whenever I get behind the wheel, a couple of miles down the road I start to think: Hmmm, I know I was worried about something. But for the life of me, I just can't remember what it was."

My Art Cars

In case you missed it, I am a car guy. That means that while other boys in my grade school class were memorizing the batting averages of their favorite baseball players, I was learning the subtle differences between taillights on 1955 and 1956 Fords. My regular readers will also have noted that I possess no mechanical aptitude whatsoever. I couldn't change a spark plug if my life depended on it. But that never dampened my car lust. I just threw myself into what I considered the most intoxicating aspect of automobiles, the styling.

Being born in 1951, the dawn of a decade of cultural excess known as the Fabulous Fifties, certainly didn't hurt. Though a mere toddler when the first tailfins sprouted on Cadillacs, by the time I hit puberty the local parking lot resembled an immense school of chrome laden road sharks complete with evil looking fins, gill slits, and leering chrome-toothed maws. The cars had the fins, but I was the one who got hooked.

Exotic magazines like *Kar Kraft* introduced me to Kustomizers like George Barris (the first guy to actually spell "custom" with a K) His creations (kreations?) like the original TV Batmobile inspired me, and my lack of mechanical ability wasn't even an issue because I had a secret weapon. I could draw!

Armed with a few paint brushes and some cans of enamel paint from Grover's Hardware, I was ready for my first Art Car project. I just needed a car. Fortunately my friend Pat Farrin was happy to offer his ancient, mud-brown Dodge (or was it a Plymouth?) as a four wheeled palette. By the time I'd finished decorating it with an assortment of random images, including a giant Lark cigarette package, I had singlehandedly transformed a forgettable old beater into something that everybody noticed. I'm not saying they liked it, just that they noticed it. Since this was all Pat and I were aiming for, we considered the project an unqualified success.

Mike Shaw must have thought so, too. The following Saturday morning he parked his tiny white Fiat 600 in the corner of my parent's driveway and when he returned on Sunday afternoon it resembled a loaf of Wonder Bread with a giant "rising sun" Japanese flag on the roof. As you'll see, the flag design was to become a signature element of my Art Car period.

Back then I held a part time job as a soda jerk at Mitchell's (later Wheeler's) Drug store. Doris Farnham stopped in one Saturday morning and casually mentioned that she was going to sell her car and somehow I talked my dad into purchasing it for me as a high school graduation gift.

Long an object of desire among local car guys, Doris's car was a pristine 1956 Chevy Bel Air. Besides being owned by the proverbial little old lady (sorry Doris), it was the rare "sports sedan" model, which meant it was a 4-door sedan with no B-pillar. Oops—sorry if I just put all you non-car-nuts to sleep. Let's just say it was a great car except that the bland two-tone paint scheme didn't look cool enough for me.

No problemo! It was time to paint my masterpiece.

I began by slathering the whole vehicle, front bumper to rear in a thick coat of white enamel house paint. No spray paint for me. I used a six-inch house painter's brush and from twenty feet away, by gorry, you could barely see the drips and brushstrokes! Once the white paint dried I had my blank canvas. So, I started painting the hood a deep blue, which somehow inspired me to leave a few large star shaped sections white. From that point on the car sort of painted itself. The sides, roof, rear fenders and trunk lid soon sported red and white stripes which almost appeared to wave as they approached the rear bumper. Cool!

Or so I thought. As it turned out, a long haired student driving a car painted like the American flag during the height of the Vietnam War generated a *whole lot* of reaction, not all of it positive!

My adventures with the American Flag Car were many and varied and I promise to explore them down the road a piece. But for now, I'll just say that I learned one very important lesson from those early art cars, one I've never forgotten. Like any artist, I'm always and solely responsible for whatever I create. However, since I first put paintbrush to fender I've been keenly aware that I'm not even remotely responsible for what you think it means.

Maine Reverse Snobbery

Keeping up with the Joneses, status seeking, upward mobility, whatever you call it, it's as American as apple pie. But just how does the desire to climb the social ladder manifest itself here in Maine? As is often the case when examining Maine culture, the answer tends to be complex, nuanced, and frequently counter intuitive.

Mainers, of course, have the same basic drive for one-up-man-ship, the same desire to appear successful in the eyes of our neighbors, as anybody else. It's just that our means and methods, not to mention some interesting notions regarding what constitutes status (a new kerosene fired generator? 150 pounds of frozen moose cutlets?) often diverge radically from mainstream trends. All of which has a tendency to baffle people from away. Which is, at least partly, the point.

Having already established that the quest for social status is a drive, why don't we start in the garage? For Americans, the path to upward mobility traditionally involves the purchase of a new car. For much of the twentieth century General Motors practically minted its own currency promoting the idea of customers relentlessly moving up the vehicular food chain. Here's how it worked. Starting with a modestly priced Chevy, you'd gradually work your way up to a more prestigious Buick or Pontiac, and if you continued to play your cards right, just about the time your eyesight, physical co-ordination, memory, and judgment drifted off into the sunset, you'd find yourself driving home in a brand new Cadillac. Following this simple script was practically a guarantee that your friends and neighbors would acknowledge that you had indeed "arrived." This was true apparently even when the only arriving that ever really happened was in your own driveway.

Meanwhile, here in Maine, where folks who lived through the Great Depression are apt to explain that it "wouldn't have been half as bad if it wun't comin' right on the heels of such hard times!", it's easy to see why conspicuous consumption never really caught on. In fact, it's a wonder to me that the phrase, "Use it up, wear it out, make it do, or do without," hasn't been incorporated into our state seal.

As a direct result of this deeply entrenched worldview, Mainers seeking elevated social status can be counted on to eschew ostentation and grandiosity in favor of frugality, practicality, and a generous dollop of Yankee ingenuity.

While style conscious denizens of Rodeo Drive feel compelled to change vehicles as frequently as the rest of us change motor oil, Mainers take a whole different tack. Think that shiny new BMW sports sedan makes you something special? Think again chummy! That fellow who just pulled into the IGA parking lot in the 1973 Monte Carlo? Well, he bought it for $100 from his great Aunt Sue who'd already put the first couple of hundred thousand miles on it, so it was just broken in when he got hold of it. When he noticed the rear fenders getting rusty he simply dug out his Sawz-all, cut it off behind the driver's seat and built a flatbed on back. It's just as comfortable, even more stylish, and now he can lug his deer back from camp without gettin' the fenders dirty. Try that in your autobahn cruiser!

A great example of Maine reverse snobbery occurred on a dirt road in Palmyra back in the early 1980s.

In those days arguably the hippest, trendiest car in Maine was a Saab 900 hatchback. Of course this was long before Subaru became the official vehicle of the Common Ground Fair and Saab passed on to that big junkyard in the sky.

So, I was more than a little surprised when Harlan Pelky, the octogenarian farmer who lived down the road from me, showed up in a brand new Saab 900 turbo. I couldn't imagine what had attracted him to such an upscale foreign car. But, as soon as he opened his mouth the mystery was solved.

According to Harlan, this shiny new Saab hatchback was the perfect vehicle for a Maine farmer. The turbocharged four-cylinder had plenty of power and didn't burn hardly any gas. Plus, with the rear seats flipped down, the hatchback up and a few strategically placed bungee cords he'd just managed to haul nearly a yard of fresh cow manure down to the back forty in it. After carrying all that manure the leather upholstery made it a snap to wash out with a garden hose. Ayuh, as far as Harlan was concerned, that little Swedish car had just put him on top of the heap, the envy of every other farmer in Somerset County.

Going East by Driving West

I have no idea whether anyone has ever actually undertaken a scientific study to determine whether visitors to Maine are any more likely to get lost than those attempting to navigate the back roads of other states. What I do know is that few, if any, states can equal Maine's reputation for quirky, confounding, and humorous direction-giving stories.

This is, of course, due in no small part to a 33 1/3 rpm record album entitled *Bert and I and Other Stories from Down East*, created by Yale students Robert Bryan and Marshall Dodge. Originally released in 1958 with a modest production run of fifty copies and a marketing strategy fueled entirely by word of mouth, that record took off like a homemade bottle rocket, launching "Maine Humor" into the stratosphere and ultimately introducing millions to the iconic phrase, "You can't get there from here."

The Bert and I album, containing dry one liners voiced in a thick Down East accent struck a chord, which soon resonated across the country and helped establish a thriving cottage industry dedicated to the promulgation, production, and distribution of authentic Maine Direction Giving Stories.

Here are a couple of classic examples of the genre:

" Does this road go all the way to Portland?"
"The road don't go nowhere, mistah. It stays right there."

"How much further to Eastport?"
"Oh, I'd say 'bout 25,000 miles the way you're headed."

One of my favorites, performed in countless venues over the past thirty plus years, involves a Labor Day weekend encounter between a summer visitor and a Mainer more than ready to see the end of tourist season.

The Mainer is sitting on the porch of the corner store minding his own business when a stranger pulls up in a vehicle with out-of-state plates, festooned with lobster trap coffee tables, giant ceramic seagull ashtrays, maple syrup, driftwood, and myriad other souvenirs of the Pine Tree State.

97

Rolling down the driver's side window he yells, "Can I take this road all the way back to New York?"

"You might just as well," quips the local. "It looks like you've got about everything else!"

Of course, growing up in Boothbay Harbor I was surrounded by masters of the art of Maine direction giving. Among the best and most prolific was my good friend the late Captain Eliot Winslow. When Captain Winslow was not piloting one of his famous tugboats or pointing out local landmarks to yet another boatload of summer folks from his perch at the helm of *The Argo*, he could often be found "numbing around the parking lot" of his lobster wharf, situated just across the Southport Island bridge from the mainland.

I was interviewing Eliot for a TV special some years back when he regaled me with one of my favorite Maine direction giving stories ever. I wish he were here to tell it, but since he's not, I'll do the honors.

According to Eliot he was standing in the Robinson's Wharf parking lot directing summer weekend tourist traffic when he noticed a sports car with out-of-state plates parked at the far end of the lot. The two male occupants were engaged in a very vocal argument, which ended abruptly when they drove way. He'd pretty much forgotten about them when they returned to the same spot about a half hour later, dug out a road map, resumed their quarrel and proceeded to drive off again. According to Eliot, "It took 'em the better part of an hour to make it back that time, so I decided perhaps they could use a little intervention."

"You boys trying to get off Southport Island?" asked Eliot. They said they were.

"Are you trying to get off Southport Island by driving west?"

"Why yes. As a matter of fact that's exactly what we've been doing."

"Well then," said Eliot, "there's your trouble. You can't get off of Southport Island by driving west. If you were to do that you'd be the first ones that's ever done it! Why don't you take a tip from an old fella who's lived around here longer than you two boys have been alive? If you want to get off this island there's only one way to do it. You'll need to head that car of yours in an easterly direction and drive back across the same bridge that you came across to get onto the island in the first place."

"But we never came across a bridge," they replied.

"Oh," says Eliot. "In that case I take it back. Your problem is . . . you ain't here yet!"

Rebel Without a Clue

I recently treated myself to a "mental health day." With my wife off visiting her family in Minnesota and the weatherman promising bright sunshine and temps in the high eighties, the conditions seemed perfect for some serious self-care.

I rose early and by six a.m. I'd fed and walked the pooch, taken out the trash, and loaded the dishwasher. Household duties duly dispatched, I headed to the garage for the ancient and mystic ritual of awakening my vintage 900 cc Honda motorcycle.

After keying the ignition, I always check to make sure the green "neutral" light is on. Then, after engaging the manual choke, I hit the starter button and stand around sipping coffee for another three or four minutes. When the engine is sufficiently warmed up, I back off the choke, reveling in the mellifluous four-cylinder symphony.

The auditory and olfactory stimulation accompanying this ritual affect me pretty much the way all that bell ringing must have affected Pavlov's dogs. I'm ready to ride.

Cruising a ribbon of fresh two-lane blacktop up near the Belgrade Lakes, I encountered plenty of other bikers with the same idea as me and couldn't help reflecting upon how far the sport of motorcycling has come since I started riding in the late sixties.

Back then the prevailing image of bikers involved scruffy leather clad outlaws out looking for trouble. But, this stereotype, reinforced in movies like the *The Wild One*, featuring Marlon Brando and Lee Marvin attempting to terrorize the good citizens of a small California town, was about to be eclipsed.

Nobody could have imagined that a scant dozen years later those bad-boy bullies would be sent packing, not by some rival motorcycle gang, but rather by a cheerful assortment of middle class housewives, Ivy League jocks, coeds, and buttoned down junior execs zipping around America on a new breed of brightly colored, inexpensive, gas sipping Japanese motorbikes. The sound track for this two-wheeled revolution

was a catchy top-forty style advertising jingle, the chorus of which promised, "You meet the nicest people on a Honda."

It should come as no surprise, then, that I took my very first motorcycle ride on one of these diminutive imports. That brief ride was all it took
to convince me I had to get my own bike. In the spring of my senior year
at high school I did just that, having finally spotted my dream machine
parked in a dusty corner of a shabby used car lot on Route 196 in Lewiston.

The bike's Ferrari red paint job and gleaming chrome tank cast a powerful spell, temporarily blinding me to its long list of less than stellar
qualities, including, but not limited too, its tiny size, skinny tires, and
conspicuous lack of anything remotely resembling actual horsepower.
Ah, but the clincher was the price. How could I possibly go wrong when
the salesman promised I could drive it off the lot for under $250, includ-
ing sales tax and fourteen-day plates? How indeed?

Did I mention the part about me driving it off the lot? Despite my
utter lack of two wheeled experience or a valid motorcycle permit, I
managed to talk the salesman into forking over the keys and my friend
Bill into driving me to Lewiston to pick it up and following me home to
make sure I got there in one piece.

Bill was one of the genuinely cool kids in town, due in large part to the
fact that he drove an electric blue Chevy Malibu 396SS, one of the hottest
muscle cars on the planet. Only years later did I realize what a ridiculous
sight the two of us must have made driving into town on that warm
spring night.

The bike I'd just spent my life savings on was a well used Honda
Sport 65, which might have hit 55 mph flat out in top gear going downhill
with a strong tailwind. At 6'3" and 200 lb., I'm sure that on the road I
resembled a Shriner who'd lost track of the original parade. Bill, following close behind me in his rumbling muscle car, only served to accentuate
the visual absurdity.

None of that mattered to me, of course. I finally had my motorcycle
and the freedom was absolutely intoxicating. Also, sad to say, it was
short lived. Within a matter of weeks the bike and I came out on the
losing end of an altercation with an octogenarian piloting a huge battleship gray Plymouth Fury.

Sadder but certainly a bit wiser, I survived the encounter with nothing more serious than a bruised ego, a broken leg, and the memory of my brief stint as a rebel without a clue.

V

A Maine Menagerie

My Maine Moose Hunt

Author's note: No moose were injured in the creation of this column.

What it is about a moose that generates such near universal appeal? A recent shopping expedition revealed standard items like books, T-shirts, calendars, bumper stickers, games, coffee mugs, caps, etc., as well as more eclectic offerings, such as milk chocolate "moose pies" (like "cow pies" only, um, edible? Ewww!) Or, for a unique north-woods fashion statement, you might try the genuine freeze-dried moose poop jewelry. I couldn't possibly make this stuff up. But for many visitors, just having a remote chance of sighting a live moose constitutes reason enough to make the trek to Maine.

If you ever do lock eyeballs with one of these gentle giants, the encounter may prove to be quite a shock. I recall back in the 70s driving two young, inner-city, UMO grad students to the coast for a lobster dinner before they headed home. Safely belted into the back seat of my compact car, they were just enjoying the fall foliage when we crested a hill and I slammed on the brakes, barely avoiding a collision with a massive cow moose standing in the middle of the road. Though stunned, my streetwise passengers didn't panic. Their urban survival instincts kicked in and they swiftly and simultaneously locked the car's rear doors.

On another occasion, CBS had approved a moose-centric "Postcard from Maine" and my producer Mary Lou Teel arranged a location shoot and some interviews up Greenville way. I interviewed one gift shop owner whose entire inventory consisted of moose themed knick knacks, including the aforementioned freeze-dried moose poop jewelry. Frankly, this struck me as having very narrow market appeal. I was assured, however, that it was extremely popular stuff. "The fellow who invented it lives just down the road," she enthused. "I'll call him if you want to talk with him." How could I refuse? I soon found myself chatting with the inventor of moose poop earrings, who described his moment of inspiration thusly: "I wuz walkin' in the woods one day when I stepped over a fallen log and my boot landed in a big pile of moose poop. I looked down and said to myself 'There must be a market for this!' " I guess that's why he's the moose poop jewelry king and you and I aren't.

All the interviews went well. But unless we located and filmed some actual moose, this postcard was never going be broadcast. That night at dinner we met the man my producer claimed could lead us to some actual moose. I was skeptical. Although a Registered Maine Guide, this fellow spoke with a thick New Jersey accent and I suspected that he'd flunked the Maine Guide test a couple of times before earning his badge. Flourishing his trusty moose call, he assured us that he could locate plenty of moose for us the following day. So we set our alarm clocks for "zero-dark-thirty" and went to bed.

The rosy fingers of the dawn found us slipping a pair of canoes into a secluded pond surround by thick forest. I was in the first with our guide. My camera crew paddled the second alongside us and Mary Lou stood on the shore directing the scene. We reached the middle of the pond and, brandishing his moose call our guide hollered, "Are you ready for the moose now?" More than ready, we gave him the OK and a long low mournful moose call echoed across the water. No response. He repeated the procedure a couple more times and we were about ready to pack it in when I noticed something big stirring along the shoreline. To my complete amazement, a pair of moose wandered out of the trees and began swimming in our direction. A moment later Mary Lou pointed to the other side of the pond where three more had decided to join the party. They proceeded to swim in our direction, munching water lilies and cavorting for the cameras as if they were all SAG/AFTA members getting time-and-a-half for the early shoot.

When the postcard aired people couldn't believe that those giant Maine moose were swimming so close to our canoes. I would have liked to explain it but you kinda had to be there.

A Boy and His Dog

There's an old saying: "If you want a friend in Washington get a dog." But why stop there? If you want a friend anyplace, a dog's a pretty good bet. That's been my experience anyway. Maybe it's just good K-9 Karma or perhaps I was brainwashed by growing up in the golden era of brilliant TV pooches like Lassie.

Back then anybody could see that Lassie was the biggest brain in the farmhouse. Heck, compared to the hopelessly dimwitted Timmy, she was MENSA material. Week after week Timmy would stumble once more into the same abandoned well while his TV mom, June Lockhart, wrung her hands and stared out the window until Lassie showed up and managed, through a complex system of whines, barks, and door scratching, to alert the humans and save the day.

I was maybe six years old when I met Deacon. He was a big, loose-jointed, endlessly affable Weimaraner with a laid-back personality and boundless enthusiasm, and we quickly formed that mystical boy-and-his-dog bond. Maybe he wasn't as smart as Lassie. But when it came to loyalty, Deacon was an army of one.

For example, in grade school I walked the mile and a half to school every day with Deacon walking beside me. When the bell rang, the students filed into the building and took our seats. The first grade classroom was on the ground floor and occasionally I'd catch Deacon peeking in the window to check on me. The pattern repeated in the second grade. The third grade, however, was a different story, the second story of the building to be precise.

We all filed into the schoolhouse via the same door we'd always used, only this time, when we got inside, we trudged upstairs to the second floor to take our seats. Caught up in the newness of third grade, I'd pretty much forgotten about Deacon. But he hadn't forgotten about me. When I heard laughter from the back of the room, I turned to see Deacon peering in through the window from his perch on the rickety old metal fire escape he'd climbed in a desperate attempt to locate his boy.

By fifth grade, Deacon was still dutifully escorting me to school, but his pattern had evolved. He'd get me safely to the front door then trot off to hobnob with his fellow wizards or whatever it is dogs do all day, occasionally checking back during recess and invariably waiting by the schoolhouse door at day's end.

One day my friend Carl asked me if I'd come to his house after school. I phoned my parents, they approved the plan, and, when school ended, I exited the building through the back door, the one used by kids like Carl who rode the bus home each day. I'm pretty sure you can see where I'm headed with this.

I was back home preparing for bed before I noticed that Deacon (who always slept at the foot of my bed) was not in the house. Panic doesn't begin to describe how I felt. I rushed off to alert the family and after a few minutes of speculation my dad said, "I know where he is." We drove to school and sure enough, there, in the moonlight, sat my faithful pal Deacon staring at the door, a door that I had entered but never exited. Hmmm, not such a dumb dog after all.

The years flew by and we both grew older. I discovered girls, cars, and rock 'n' roll and spent more and more time away from home and Deacon reluctantly abandoned his secret service job. But he'd always meet me, his tail wagging enthusiastically, as I arrived home at the end of each school day.

Deacon lived to a ripe old age, passing quietly in his sleep when I was in my mid teens. It was a terrible day but by then I was well on my way into the big wide world, where, more often than not, you can't bring your dog anyway.

I've had some really great dogs since then. But, none will ever replace Deacon in that secret place deep in my heart. For more than two decades after his passing he appeared to me in a recurring dream. It was always the same. I'd awake into a dream landscape frightened, alone, confused, and anxious. Then I'd call Deacon's name and he'd come bounding across a field of bright summer flowers, young and strong, all tail wags and boundless joy. Somehow I always awoke from one of those dreams to a safer more comforting world. Now, I ask you, who could ask for a better friend than that?

A Cats' Tale

If you happen to encounter a public service announcement on TV wherein I'm earnestly encouraging you to adopt a homeless cat, you shouldn't be too surprised. I have a real soft spot for animals in general and over the years I've taken home my share, well let's be honest, *more* than my share of stray cats.

For several years I was involved with a non-profit organization dedicated to finding homes for abandoned, stray, and homeless felines. As you might suspect, in the course of acquiring and redistributing all those kitties, I managed to collect quite a few memorable cat tales as well.

One of my favorite stories began innocently enough when a lady in a nearby trailer park phoned to say that her neighbor, recently departed for that big doublewide in the sky, had left behind four near-feral cats huddled in the crawlspace beneath his trailer. She'd been in contact with the man's family and they were anxious to have us remove the displaced felines ASAP.

You're familiar with the phrase "herding cats"? Well, as someone who has actually done it, I can report that it's every bit as frustrating as it sounds. Fortunately the right combination of patience, canned tuna, and have-a-heart traps will usually do the trick.

Lacking the resources to maintain a full-time shelter, we had lined up several volunteers willing to provide foster homes for cats awaiting a more permanent placement. This system worked well enough as long as the cats were already at least somewhat domesticated. Problems did arise, however, when dealing with near feral cats like the trailer park refugees.

Somehow we managed to find an older couple willing to take in all four cats. Unfortunately, shortly after arrival they vanished into thin air, only to reappear a day or so later hiding in the dark recesses of a bedroom closet, refusing to come out even to eat!

Basically it was a stand off. Those cats had barely managed to develop a relationship with *one* human being. As far as they were concerned, the rest of us could just butt out! Casting about for clues as to how to proceed, we contacted the former neighbor to see if she had any suggestions.

Not to put too fine a point on it, she explained that her neighbor had been, by all accounts, a plain old-fashioned blackout drunk, whose alcoholic condition dictated a routine that required getting plastered at his favorite local tavern six nights out of seven. Apparently on the seventh day he rested, preferring to spend his Sundays boozing in the privacy of his own trailer, surrounded by his four feline friends and listening to several hours of "preacher shows" on TV.

This last bit of information didn't require much snooping on the part of the neighbor, since everybody in the trailer park could hear him singing along at top volume to gospel favorites like the "Old Rugged Cross" and "Shall We Gather at The River?" I didn't see how this detail would help us with the cats. But I passed it along to our volunteer couple just in case.

A week or so later we heard from them, this time with an unexpectedly upbeat report. The cats, they informed us with no small amount of pride, had been making a remarkably speedy adjustment to life with their human housemates, venturing out of the closet to eat, explore, use the litter box, and even take an occasional catnap on the sunny window ledge.

My inquiry as to how they'd made such amazing progress was met with a chuckle and an invitation to visit. If I'd stop by, they assured me, they would reveal the secret of their success.

My curiosity was certainly piqued. When I stopped by later that day, they ushered me upstairs and, sure enough, all four cats were settling in nicely, far more relaxed and happy than I would have thought possible just a few days earlier. How on earth had this miracle been accomplished?

That's when I noticed a battered boom-box style audio cassette player sitting on a card table in the corner of the room. Stepping over for a closer look I began to wonder whether perhaps there really had been a spiritual component to the "miracle of the cats." I popped the audio cassette out of the tape player and read the label: *Gospel Greats! America's Most Loved Songs of Praise by the Original Artists.*

People always seem to wonder whether dogs go to heaven. I have no idea, of course. But, at that moment I was pretty sure I knew of four cats who were headed in the right direction.

The Young Man and the Sea

Last week I ran into my childhood friend Bill at the drug store. Bill and I know each other the way you can only know someone you've shared a dozen or so grade school classrooms with. I'm not sure sitting in rows of ancient, uncomfortable, hand carved (by generations of former students) school desks year after year made us close, but I know Bill and Bill knows me in a way that folks who don't have our shared experience could never understand. One thing I know about Bill is that ever since sometime around the third grade he knew that the only thing he ever wanted to be was a lobsterman. Not surprisingly, given that single-minded career path, he's been hauling "crawlers" on the Maine coast his whole adult life.

Bill was glad to see me but looking a little down at the mouth. When I asked how things were going he sighed and commented on the depressed market price for lobster this season, "Hardly pays for the gas to go get 'em," he muttered. "But I still do." Of course he does. For folks like Bill and me there never was a Plan B. We do what we do, come what may, good times or bad, because it's just that, what we do. The good news is that makes us pretty much immune to unemployment. That's right. Folks like me and Bill may not have a paycheck this week but by gorry we'll always have a job!

Seeing him brought to mind the amazing true story of my own first experience stalking the Maine lobster.

Arriving on the Maine coast fresh from the endless potato fields of northern Aroostook County, my youthful summers quickly became a blur of mackerel fishing, clam digging, messing about in boats, swimming, and climbing around on massive granite boulders. I spent hours studying green crabs, limpets, minnows, periwinkles, and myriad other exotic denizens of the tide pool. But my favorite spot of all was the float at the end of the pier at Sample's Shipyard, where I could stretch out in the sun, peer into the briny deep and observe the underwater inhabitants of a barnacle encrusted rock pile. I fished there for cunner and pollack and proudly lugged home my catch. The lugging home part actually turned out to be short lived. It ended pretty abruptly when my mom instituted a strict "eat whatever you catch" policy. Trust me on this, one big serving of boney cunner with a side of fried eel will make anyone join the catch-and-release movement.

One afternoon, as I sprawled on the dock dangling a clam-baited hook in front of a rocky outcropping, I noticed a pair of greenish brown claws edging toward it and realized there was a lobster less than six inches from my hook! From that moment on I was obsessed with catching it. If there's a Guinness world record for this sort of thing I'm pretty sure I'd win because, seriously, who else would even enter?

Like a pre-adolescent Don Quixote I began my quest with that boundless energy that seems the special province of genius inventors and ten-year-old boys. Day after day I returned to my task with a freshly refined strategy. I tried dozens of baits, from a half eaten PB&J sandwich to sun-dried periwinkles. I experimented with letting him drag the bait into his cave and then swiftly hauling him to the surface, a brilliant tactic until he broke the surface and simply let go and swam home. How embarrassing!

Word of my battle got around and a steady stream of workmen and tourists stopped to watch. Despite encouragement from onlookers I'd almost given up when I began hauling in my line one afternoon and felt a steady resistance on the other end. Had I snagged the hook? Nope. I tugged and it kept coming. Suddenly, I saw my lobster break the surface flipping and flapping for all he was worth only this time he couldn't let go. I'd hooked him as surely as ever a fish was hooked.

I was so shocked! Fortunately a nearby workman emptied a bag of stove bolts and hollered, "Put him in here." I stuffed my catch in the bag and ran home. I'm not sure whether anybody actually ever bought my story of having caught a Maine lobster right off the dock on a hook and line. But frankly, I couldn't have cared less. I knew the truth and that's all that mattered. Oh yeah, and that night at supper the eat-what-you-catch rule was just fine by me.

The Fish Whisperer

It should come as no surprise to readers of my work that I like to fish. Perhaps you recall an account describing my youthful, and ultimately successful, quest to hook a lobster on a hand line. Clearly, I'm not picky about my gear or the species of fish I catch. If it's got fins (or even a pair of claws) I'm onboard or on the shoreline or the dock as the case may be.

Of the saltwater varieties, I've managed to land everything from mackerel to flounder, including oddities like cunner, sculpin, dogfish, and the occasional eel or squid. My fresh-water experience runs to common varieties of bass, perch, and pickerel. When I was old enough to follow the necessary arcane rituals involved, my dad taught me about fly-fishing, the better to lure the wily brook trout to my line. Alas, thus far that species has proven too wily to fall (or jump) for my amateurish fly-casting attempts.

Nevertheless, I continue to enjoy fishing. So, upon learning that my youngest sister-in-law was an angler, I naturally assumed that fishing would be a fun activity we could enjoy together. That naive notion evaporated on our very first fishing trip.

I quickly discovered that going fishing with Charlotte is like going bird watching with St. Francis of Assisi. I mean let's say that by some miracle you *did* arrange for such an outing, just you and old St. Francis hiking into the pucker brush with your binoculars and a well-worn Peterson guide.

You, of course, would be expecting to watch the birds. The birds on the other hand, vast flocks of them no doubt, would presumably be arriving from miles around to hang out with their special pal, the Saint. That's pretty much what it's like to spend a few hours angling with my sister-in-law Charlotte—the Fish Whisperer.

I'll give you an example and let you draw your own conclusions. The following is a factual account of a morning I spent fishing with my sister-in-law.

The Fish Whisperer was visiting us in Maine and we spent some time at our camp in Washington County. We're located on a lake known for its excellent bass fishing, and early one morning we tossed our gear in the boat and headed for a secluded cove where I'd had pretty good luck in the past.

We dropped anchor, baited our hooks, cast our lines into the water and commenced that age-old angler's pastime, waiting for a nibble. It seemed to me that everything was going along well since we actually got quite a few nibbles and even landed a couple of fish in the first hour or so. But I could tell that my sister-in-law was less than thrilled, so I asked her if anything was bothering her. She responded by asking if I minded her offering a few suggestions on my fishing technique. Ever the good host I told her by all means, offer away.

What happened next unfolded like a scene from one of those Kung Fu movies, wherein the ancient and venerated master shows the acolytes why he's boss and they're not. Sitting trancelike in the center of the boat, eyebrows furrowed, eyes flashing, the Fish Whisperer methodically surveyed the cove. Having decided upon a course of action, she abruptly lifted an oar and sculled us about six feet closer to shore, stopped, peered into the depths as if consulting a submerged crystal ball, then moved the boat another foot and half to starboard and dropped anchor.

She then commenced to dictate exceptionally precise instructions regarding hook size, bobber, and worm placement, depth, drift angle, and god knows what else. All I can say is that I did exactly what she said to do and the results were amazing.

Within seconds we each had a whopper bass on the line and for the next two hours the fish kept coming at a staggering rate. I always follow a catch-and-release policy, but the Fish Whisperer took it a few steps further. Her approach was more like "catch-unhook-photograph-kiss-and-release!"

Yep. Not only does she keep a precise written and photographic log of each fish she's caught and where she caught it (sort of like Facebook, only underwater), she also gives each one a gentle goodbye kiss before releasing it.

Laugh all you want. We hauled in 67 fish before lunch and although all bass look pretty much alike to me, I suspect that there were a few that morning who went for the hook a second or even a third time in order to spend a few more precious moments with the Fish Whisperer!

Good Dog!

Ever notice how everybody seems to think *their* dog is a cut above average, the cutest, brightest, pooch that ever walked God's green earth? I sure have.

Oddly enough, folks often make this dubious claim at the very moment old Spot himself is leaving his doggie calling card on *your* patch of green earth, suggesting rather strongly that such blind faith in your dog's elemental goodness is rarely justified.

Be that as it may, you won't find me sharing this observation with Mary Jane while we're standing around chatting and her "simply adorable" pit bull is snarling menacingly, straining at his leash, anxious to amputate my hand should I wander within range. "Go ahead," she gushes. "You can pet him. He's really very friendly." Um, if it's all the same to you M.J., I'll just take your word for it.

The truth is, I'm as guilty of selective canine blindness as anyone. Many years ago I had a huge, male Akita/wolf mix. He was a magnificent animal and, in his later years, Killer (Not his real name but not wildly inappropriate either) was so docile he'd allow kittens to romp on his ears and playfully pummel his massive snout. Only close friends and family members knew the darker truth—if there's any validity to the claim that all dogs go to heaven, Killer was destined to be re-united with several he'd sent along ahead of him.

Another dog of mine, Bridget, an affable, one-year-old Irish Setter with a brain the size of a walnut, was in pretty rough shape when she arrived at my doorstep. Although she'd been seriously neglected and underfed, she quickly responded physically to a simple regimen of good food, indoor lodging, exercise, and attention. Her behavioral issues, on the other hand, would clearly require more work.

Not to put too fine a point on it, Bridget's behavior was appalling. Forget "sit," "stay," and "rollover." This barely house-broken, fifty-pound, canine rocket sled would charge through the front door, careen around the house like Rin Tin Tin on bath salts, leap onto the kitchen table and proceed to scarf down anything remotely edible. Everything from a loaf of Wonder bread (still in its plastic wrapper) to the Thanks-giving turkey was up for grabs.

Never a believer in corporal punishment for man or beast, I chose to employ a gentler reward-based regimen with an emphasis on unwaver-ing consistency over the long term. I'm pleased to report that it worked. Well, it sort of worked, as you will soon see.

I assure you that if you're willing to invest all your patience and enough cash for a year's supply of dog biscuits, even a dog with a wal-nut-size brain can acquire the basics of civilized house pet etiquette. Please note my use of the word "basics."

Still tragically behind the curve in the gray matter department, Brid-get nonetheless mastered all of them. She would enthusiastically sit, stay, speak, and roll over on cue from sunup to sundown, or as long as the dog biscuits held out anyway.

I felt fully justified taking pride in what was, after all, an epic canine success story. Alas, as the good book says, such pride inevitably "goeth before a fall." Unbeknownst to me, my fall was lurking right around the corner.

One warm spring morning, Bridget was snoozing on her dog bed in the living room when I heard the postman pull up to my mailbox. Just as I was preparing to step out the door, I remembered the glass pie plate filled with graham cracker crust, sitting on my kitchen table.

It had been well over a year since Bridget last pulled one of her old leaping-on-the-table stunts, so, glancing at her napping innocently in the warm sunshine, I decided to risk leaving her alone, briefly, with the pie crust while I dashed out for the mail.

I wasn't gone two minutes. Upon my return I noted with satisfaction that Bridget was still curled up asleep on her bed. She hadn't moved an inch! As I carried the mail over to table and set it down, I noticed the empty pie plate. Not a crumb of graham cracker crust remained. Shining as if it had just emerged from the rinse cycle, the glass had been licked perfectly clean.

I turned back toward Bridget, still apparently asleep with one eye-brow slightly arched, and grudgingly acknowledged that yes indeed, walnut brain notwithstanding, my very own dog had somehow managed to cleverly pull off the perfect dog crime. Clearly *my* dog must be a cut above average, the cutest, brightest canine on God's green earth. Hmmm, I thought, "Good Dog."

Elver Maine-ia!

I almost swallowed my Trident gum when I stumbled upon a recent news story listing the astronomical figure of $1800 per pound as the market price of a commodity for which, until recently, most Mainers wouldn't have paid you a buck a barrel. I am of course referring to elvers.

Having had the good fortune of growing up on the Maine coast, I know something about elvers. I have fond childhood memories of warm spring evenings spent scooping alewives (and, unintentionally, the occasional pound of elvers) by hand from the swiftly moving, brackish stream that runs beneath Route 27 connecting a tidal estuary on the seaward side to the southern shore of West Harbor Pond.

Not up to speed on these slippery investment grade aquatic kruger-rands? According to that fount of crowd-sourced wisdom, Wikipedia, elvers, a.k.a. glass eels, are an early stage version of *Anguilla rostrata* , ". . . a facultative catadromous fish found on the east coast of North America." But, you already knew that much, right?

Actually maybe you did. It turns out that "catadromous" is just a fancy way of saying that elvers migrate from fresh to salt water when they're all het up and ready to get out into the big ocean and spawn. Come to think of it, that sort of behavior is popular with a number of species found in Maine.

When you stop to think about it, these tiny transparent baby eels (a whopper elver would be around 3½ inches) are just the latest in a long line of culinary rarities to be discovered and harvested on the Maine coast. Like sea urchins, mussels, periwinkles, and similar critters, elvers, for reasons far beyond my comprehension, are a highly prized gastronomic delicacy in certain far-flung corners of the globe. I know. Go figure, right?

Having personally encountered vast numbers of elvers (not that difficult given that momma eels give birth to about four million offspring annually), I must confess that it has never occurred to me to chow down on a mess of them baked, boiled, broiled, fried, or (ewww!) raw, which is apparently the method preferred by true elver lovers. But maybe that's just me. Frankly, I feel pretty much the same way about smelts.

On the other hand, who in their right mind is going to argue with someone offering $1800 a pound for baby eels, several million of which during the spring no doubt swim around in some random inlet a mile or so from your front porch? And though locals have precious little interest in eating the critters, the cash infusion from the annual elver harvest certainly helps put food on the table for a lot of Maine families. And like I said, this is nothing new. We've seen this movie before.

If fact, when I was growing up, every school kid in Maine was taught that back in Colonial times, lobsters were so plentiful that they could be found washed up on the shore in huge drifts following a storm. Old timers back then told colorful, highly improbable sounding tales about lobsters being so common folks used them for fertilizer.

Summer visitors paying premium prices for "shore dinners" in Maine's upscale restaurants would be shocked to discover that a couple hundred years ago eating lobsters was considered a sign of poverty and associated with indentured servitude. According to the Lobster Institute, servants in one village in the early Massachusetts Colony eventually got fed up with the situation and successfully petitioned the local magistrate for a legal writ guaranteeing they'd not be fed lobster more than thrice weekly!

And really, if you think about it, how hungry would you have to be to encounter a lobster crawling along a rocky ledge and think, "Hmmm, I bet if I threw that thing in a pot full of boiling water for twenty minutes or so it'd make a tasty dinner"? Pretty hungry I'm thinking.

All of which brings me to the following question. If elvers are only the latest in a long line of weird Maine seafood specialties that somebody, someplace is willing to swap great bags of cash for, what's next on the list?

Based on past experience I'd say that whoever figures that one out stands a better than average chance of becoming a millionaire. It's worth thinking about, don't you agree? What's it gonna be? Sea slugs? Barnacles?

Given the abundant variety of marine life in the Gulf of Maine, the list is a long one. The only real problem will involve finding someone brave enough to taste test your latest recipe.

How to Eat a Lobster

Perhaps you've noticed that just as the weather has begun to cool in the waning days of summer, the rhetoric in the long running feud between Maine lobstermen and their Canadian rivals is heating up. Don't worry, I won't be jumping (literally or figuratively) into the middle of a disagreement between rival gangs of lobstermen. I've had enough first hand experience with lobstermen to know that they tend to be precisely the sort of tough, pragmatic, rugged individualists you wouldn't want to pick *any sort* of fight with, particularly one that involves the manner in which they choose to make their living.

Let's face it, lobstermen have been hauling traps and hurling insults (among other things) across the border at one another for about as long as anybody can remember. If there were a simple solution to this longstanding maritime squabble, somebody would have sorted it out by now.

So I won't weigh in on the Maine/Canadian lobster spat. In fact, I only brought it up because it involves different approaches to the harvesting and marketing of soft shell and hard shell lobsters, and the soft shell/hard shell brouhaha is a whole other kettle of shellfish! One about which, like a lot of Mainers, I have plenty of opinions.

Of course, not everyone considers the prospect of making a meal of a lobster to be a particularly enticing proposition. Honestly, can you blame them? Even a lifelong lobster lover such as myself must ultimately concede that one's first encounter with a steaming, fresh-out-of-the-pot *Homerus americanus* staring balefully up at you from a dinner plate is liable to be a tad off-putting. No doubt, the prospect of breaking and entering the rock-hard carapace of a critter that, until about two o'clock yesterday afternoon, was minding its own business crawling along the ocean floor, takes a little getting used too. Nor am I one of those judgmental types who view failure to appreciate this Maine delicacy as a sign of moral turpitude. It's simply a choice. But, I believe that it should at least be an *informed* choice. Here's what I mean:

For a decade or so, Dan Gianneshi was my regular soundman for my Postcards from Maine essays on CBS. Prior to working in Maine, Danny's experience with lobsters had been almost exclusively influenced by stuffy, overpriced, upscale urban eateries. No wonder he wasn't impressed.

That all changed the first time I took him out for a meal at the Boothbay Region Lobsterman's Co-op. The pure joy of bellying up to a picnic table with a spectacular water view to chow down on fresh Maine lobster while dressed in jeans and a sweatshirt was a revelation.

It didn't take him long to figure out that tearing into a lobster using his bare hands, with no fear of embarrassing himself in front of his friends or generating a massive dry cleaning bill for that rented tux, was a real game changer. From then on, any Maine video shoot with Dan commenced with a visit to the nearest lobster wharf.

Having established that atmosphere is a critical aspect of any successful lobster feed, it's time to take the crustacean by the claws and tackle the perennial soft shell-vs.-hard shell controversy.

In terms of Maine culinary lore, this controversy ranks right up there with the epic crumbs-vs.-batter fried clam debate (another story for another day), and people certainly have different tastes. So, there's really no right or wrong answer.

Wait a minute! What am I saying? Of course there's a right answer. Hard shell lobsters are far better than those wimpy soft shells any day! Here's why: basic Lobster 101 teaches us that lobsters achieve their growth by the periodic shedding of a protective outer shell. This means that a lobster that is almost ready to shed (the hard shell stage) yields nearly twice as much meat as one that has recently slipped into a new (soft) shell. For a lobster lover like me, that makes hard shell the obvious choice. As far as I can tell, the whole point of the soft shell lobster is that it's easier to break into.

Really? What fun is that? Should we simply abandon our vaunted Puritan work ethic so easily? I think not. I was raised to believe that anything worth having is worth working for. So I'll take my lobster with the hardest shell available, thank you very much, the harder the better.

Oh, in case you were wondering why I insist on keeping a hammer in my silverware drawer? Well, now you know.

VI

Oh, the People You'll Meet

Stern Man

I was sixteen years old when my dad, a great believer in the virtues of me doing hard work, talked me into taking a job as stern man on a lobster boat. The lobsterman, I'll call him Arlo (not his real name), lived in East Boothbay, which in those days was only remotely akin to living in Booth-bay Harbor—that goes for Boothbay, Trevett and Barter's Island too. Even now, when people say, "So you're from Boothbay," I correct them. "Nope. I'm from Boothbay Harbor." A different thing entirely.

Arlo fished a traditional wooden-hulled boat and believed that if God had wanted us to have fiberglass boats, He would have made fiberglass trees. He'd pick me up at four a.m. and drive to the dock. By 4:30 we'd be pitching rotting redfish carcasses into bait tubs. If you weren't fully awake at this point, the stench would do the trick. We cast off and headed for the open ocean before sun-up. Barely a word was spoken the entire time. Arlo might offer a mumbled, "Munin'," as I got into his truck but basically compared to him, the man of few words is a regular chatterbox, so we stood silently on deck smoking cigarettes in the pre-dawn dark.

Sunrise found us a mile or two offshore hauling strings of six heavy wooden traps, backbreaking work with little room for error. Arlo would ease the boat to within a few feet of a jagged rock cliff, feathering the throttle with one hand while holding the gaff in the other. Then he'd snag the buoy, haul it in, and wrap the line around the winch hanging out-board over the starboard rail. Then he'd kick it into high gear, the engine whine rising a notch. As the boat rocked to starboard the line grew taught, sizzling up from the depths and flinging a fine salt mist in my face. When the first trap surfaced I was on it, hoisting it aboard, opening the door, tossing sculpins, sea snails, and urchins overboard. I'd measure and toss back the shorts and breeders, heaving the keepers into a crate at the stern. That winch was still cranking full throttle as I slid the baited trap onto the transom just as the next one arrived.

Baiting these old wooden traps went like this: open the trap, take the bait iron (like a long darning needle with a hole in the sharp end), thread a cord through the eye of the iron, ram it straight through the empty eye sockets of a half dozen stinking redfish, then hang the bait inside. All six traps were arranged on the fantail so at full throttle they'd fly off in rapid succession like a line of paratroopers. At around noon we'd break to scarf down a couple of sandwiches and a Coke. We sat on the transom, eating in silence, staring at the endless sea and sky, not socializin', just takin' a lunch break. Then back at it. Hard.

As the summer flew by I grew stronger and more confident, made good money, and even managed to save some of it, due mostly to the fact that I couldn't stay awake past 6 p.m. Soon enough, the third week of August rolled around and the football coach, perhaps noticing my newly acquired muscles, asked me to join the team. I asked Arlo about getting done a couple of weeks early and in an uncharacteristic burst of verbal enthusiasm he said, "Ayuh, that'll be okay" — or words to that effect.

My last day as a stern man was one of those postcard-gorgeous Maine days. Around noon, however, the engine abruptly shut down and I thought, "Hmm, this isn't a good sign." Offering no explanation, Arlo snagged one of our buoys, rigged a makeshift mooring, ducked down the hatchway, and rummaged around in the galley, emerging a moment later with a battered metal cook pot. He fastened a line to the handle, tossed it over the side and brought it back half-full of seawater. As he lit the galley stove and put the pot on to boil, I was starting to get the idea. Grinning at me for the first time ever he asked, "Just how many of these crawlers you s'pose you can eat, anyway?" I was caught off-guard. That was an incredibly long speech for Arlo.

"Oh, I dunno, maybe two or three?"

He snatched a half-dozen lobsters, tossed them into the pot of steaming water, sat down opposite me, and lighting a cigarette, began to talk. He told me I'd done a darned good job as his stern man. That took more words than he'd used all summer, but he didn't stop there. He asked me about my plans. Was I going to play football for the Seahawks? I can't recall his questions, much less my answers, but I'll never forget the way I felt that afternoon. Sitting on deck in the late summer sun, it dawned on me that we were just talking like men talk to one another, easy, relaxed, man to man. It was a new and marvelous sensation.

We ate our fill, casually tossing lobster shells over the side, as a growing flock of gulls materialized from nowhere to fight over the remains. One last cup of coffee and a smoke and Arlo fired up the engine and headed in. Back at the dock after unloading the catch, stowing the gear, and hosing down the boat for the last time, Arlo reached out and shook my hand. His felt like a rough chunk of rock maple. He looked me right in the eye and said, "If you ever want to be a stern man again, you come see me."

I never did. If nothing else, that summer motivated me to pursue a career that didn't involve hard physical labor. I did, however, stop by and visit him a few times over the years. He was always hard at work so the visits were short and although he never said so, I could just tell that he was genuinely pleased to see me. That silent message, coming from a Maine lobsterman, is high praise indeed.

Stories You Tell Me

One nice side benefit of my job as a humorist is that I occasionally get to perform at spiffy upscale resorts like Ocean Reef Club in Key Largo, Florida. It's no secret that a few days of Florida sunshine around mud season can do wonders for any winter weary Mainer, and it doesn't hurt that there's a paycheck involved.

The audience at my most recent Ocean Reef appearance was composed mostly of people from away, a fairly high percentage of whom either maintain a summer home in Maine or have at least visited a time or two. Following the performance I experienced an odd but not entirely uncommon phenomenon. Having just spent an hour or so listening to *my* Maine stories, audience members began cueing up to tell me *their* Maine stories. Although the quality of these yarns varies widely, every now and then a real gem like this one emerges.

My interlocutor, a Massachusetts native who'd once spent a year working in Bethel, Maine, told me that he'd been impressed with the small town ambience and rich assortment of colorful characters he'd encountered there.

When the year ended his company recalled him to the home office and as he was packing for the move, he noticed that the automatic transmission on his vintage Mercedes sedan had suddenly begun slipping badly. Purchased new, the car had been regularly maintained by the dealership's service department, currently not so conveniently located some two hundred miles away. Thus, on the morning of his departure, he found himself all packed up and effectively stranded in his driveway in Bethel.

Despite serious doubts as to whether the grease monkey at the local filling station/garage could effect a proper repair on such exotic machinery, he was fresh out of other options, so he made the call.

"Ayuh, I 'magine I can give 'er a look-see anyway," came the quick reply, somewhat garbled by a mouthful of Italian sandwich no doubt washed down with a swig or two of Moxie. "But, 'twon't be fer anothah half ow-ah yet. Gotta finish eatin' m' lunch."

127

In due time the mechanic hove into view clad in faded oil stained over-alls and lugging his battered toolbox. Once the problem had been explained, Mr. Fix-it set aside the toolbox and slid under the chassis for the promised look-see. Following a minute or two of grunting and groaning, he slithered back into the sunlight, stood up, wiped his hands on an oily rag, and, nodding to our friend, said, "There. Give 'er a try now."

More than a little dubious, the owner slid in behind the wheel, cranked the starter and put the car in gear. To his amazement it moved forward effortlessly, no lag, no slipping transmission, no problem. Truly impressed, he asked, "What did you do?"

"Fixed it, didn't I?" came the laconic response.

Payment having been offered and declined, the local man wished him safe travel, grabbed his toolbox, and headed back downtown, presumably to spend the afternoon pumping gas, giving directions, and catching the last half of the Red Sox game on the radio.

Both car and driver made it home without further problems and my storyteller had almost forgotten the whole incident until a few months later when he'd brought the car to the Mercedes dealership for an oil change.

Suddenly recalling the impromptu repair made by a shade tree mechanic up in Maine, he recounted the tale to the service manager. "Since you've got it in for service anyway," he asked, "would you mind taking a look underneath just to see if you can figure out how that fellow managed to fix my transmission in under two minutes without using any of his tools?"

A few minutes later he was summoned from the waiting room and escorted into the service bay. With the car perched on a hydraulic lift, the manager used a long screwdriver to point out a flange on the bottom of the transmission housing where a large bolt should have been. The bolt was missing in action. But, in its place, holding the transmission housing together were a half dozen or so plastic coated metal twist-ties of the sort generally used to re-seal bread wrappers after they've been opened.

Mechanical mystery solved! The transmission of this classic Mercedes, a marvel of German engineering, had been performing flawlessly for several months on the strength of a repair improvised on the spot by a small town Maine mechanic in under two minutes, utilizing only raw Yankee ingenuity and materials found in the pockets of his overalls! And to think that people still ask me where I get my material.

Down East Deadpan

Some time ago I received a voice mail message from Terry Jr., our contractor, carpenter, and all 'round build-it, fix-it, tear-it-down-and-haul-it-off guy who lives a few miles down the road from our camp in Washington County. Terry Jr. is in the process of taking over more and more of his dad's (Terry Sr.) well established carpentry business up in our neck of the eastern Maine woods.

As far as I can tell, though young in years, the son is cut from the same bolt of cloth as the father. His work certainly bears a family resemblance to the old man's. It's simple, solid stuff featuring a common sense, form-follows-function design and a level of quality that reflects genuine pride in his work He's also clearly adopted his dad's dry, deadpan, "Down East" sense of humor.

One of the first projects Terry Sr. did for us after we purchased the camp was to build us a new dock in his workshop and install it on our little patch of lakefront. He and the adult sons plus a youthful nephew or two were on hand to help with the launching, which involved floating the new dock a few hundred yards from the public landing to our property. As his makeshift crew poled and paddled the awkward structure along the shore, the scene resembled something out of *Tom Sawyer* and *Huckleberry Finn*. It was a lovely early summer day with sun sparkling off the placid lake as the younger kids splashed around having a fine old adventure. Terry Sr. stood on the bank directing the operation with a critical eye. When the dock was finally, safely installed, one of the younger kids just couldn't resist the urge to leap fully clothed into the lake. "Hey!" Terry hollered. "What do you think you're doing?" Chastened, the boy replied, "Well, I figured after all this work I deserved a swim." Terry's deadpan response was, "Who says you've done any work?"

Back here in the future, I returned Terry Jr's call. He informed me that he was about halfway done with his current project so he'd need to get some more money to keep going. I took down the numbers and asked how the project (remodeling the bathroom) was coming along. "Well," he said in a monotone as flat as your palm, "when we tore off the wall paneling to get at the pipes the whole camp collapsed." I'll admit that my brain waves hit a mental frost heave for a second or two. But I bounced right back, grinning into the phone and said, "Yeah, well, that'll happen sometimes."

"Ayuh," said Terry Jr., "it will." The brief exchange was classic Down-East-deadpan delivery. I was tickled and also relieved that I was the one having this conversation with him rather than my wife. She's a Minnesota girl not a native Mainer, and even after more than twenty-five years in the Pine Tree State she's still prone to fall straight into one of these home-grown Maine humor conversational booby traps when chatting with the locals.

I suppose the fact that I grew up with this sort of homespun local entertainment must have influenced my decision to pursue a career as a Maine humorist. I mean how many times did I overhear Brud Pierce (the hot-dog king) breaking the sad news to some unwitting tourist that the town fathers had made a fateful decision regarding the famous foot-bridge across the inner harbor. Brud intoned morosely, "Ayuh, they've finally decided they aren't going to have it any longer." Just when the hapless patron was digging out her camera for one last snapshot of the landmark before it was torn down, Brud would grin and add (drum roll please), "Nope, they figure it's long enough just as it is!"

About twenty years back I was down at Skip Cahill's Tire on the Old Bath Road. I'd purchased a set of tires from one of the big national tire warehouse companies and Skip had mounted and balanced them for me. It didn't seem to bother him that I hadn't purchased the tires from him so I went on my way without giving it any more thought. For some reason though, that set of tires seemed to be cursed. I picked up a nail in one of them less than a week after Skip put them on my car. A few weeks later there was some curb rash on another, which necessitated replacement of yet another almost brand new tire. Skip always got me right in and did the work promptly and professionally with nary a hint of editorial comment. I can't recall what the exact problem was with tire number three, but it happened just a week or two later and I wasn't too happy to be making one more trip to Cahill's and shelling out another hefty chunk of change to put things right. As I stood by the fender watching Skip re-mount yet another of my bargain tires, I grumbled, "Boy, I'm just having the worst darned luck I've ever had with this set of tires." "Ayuh," says Skip. "That'll happen with these national chain store tires." The line was, of course, delivered without a hint of inflection, no remonstrance for my failure to shop locally, no subtle, "I told you so"—nope. Just a good dose of good-for-what-ails-ya Down East deadpan, straight from the horse's mouth.

By the way, if anybody tries to tell you that this sort of classic dry Yankee repartee is going out of style, I recommend the following response, "That depends on who you talk too."

Psychic Carpentry

Like most folks, you probably consider the building trades to be among the most practical of all jobs. Whether nailing together a potting shed or erecting a vast Victorian pile, the nuts and bolts of construction are just that, nuts and bolts, hammers and nails, hard, physical materials. But, if you're looking for a carpenter in Down East Maine, you'd be well advised to familiarize yourself with the more metaphysical aspects of the profession, at least as important to the success of your project as any of the actual laws of physics.

When we purchased our camp Down East it was reasonably sound structurally, but very much in need of a complete cosmetic overhaul. The walls sported acres of fake wood paneling that, along with avocado-tone appliances, had seriously threatened to engulf American interiors back in the mid-seventies. So we hired a highly recommended local carpenter to do the renovations and he agreed that knotty pine throughout would be a good solution. Everything was going just fine until we mentioned that we thought we'd be leaving the small, dowdy kitchen with its cheesy cabinets as-is for the time being. Suddenly his sunny mood turned dark and I swear I could hear that faint, high, eerie "woo-woo" music that TV shows use to indicate the presence of restless spirits. Thus began our first visit to the Twilight Zone of Maine psychic carpentry.

Without going into the details (which seem strangely impossible to recall anyway), I'll just say that when the sawdust settled we were the proud owners of a renovated kitchen featuring gorgeous handmade pine cabinets with granite beach stone drawer pulls. It was exactly what we'd wanted, except we didn't know we wanted it. We didn't, but our psychic carpenter did! That's the essence of psychic carpentry. But please don't make the mistake of confusing this with upselling, bait and switch, or any of those other high-pressure big city sales techniques. No, Ma'am. Psychic carpentry is not about gouging the customer. Often the result is actually less expensive than what you originally had in mind. No, it's all about intuiting dreams and desires hidden in your subconscious. Our psychic carpenter is sort of like the horse whisperer. Maybe I should refer to him as "the house whisperer." Whatever it is, he has an absolutely uncanny knack of knowing what we want and need, even (especially) when we haven't got a clue.

A couple of summers back we innocently suggested that he build us a simple stockade type fence on the southern edge of our property. Outwardly, he seemed open to that option, even going so far as to jot down a few notes on the back of an envelope, promising to look into the cost of materials and give us an estimate. On the psychic plane though, something completely different was happening. It was like a scene in one of those spooky movies where the ghost person inside a character separates from the physical body and moves around independently. While his physical body was jotting down notes and nodding agreeably, our carpenter's psychic body was kneeling in the dirt, mumbling arcane incantations and drawing mystical symbols in the dirt.

The upshot was that many months went by without any more talk (or action) regarding our simple stockade fence plan. Summer turned to fall, fall to winter, winter to spring, with nary a sign of the fence. We had all but despaired of ever seeing it and were even considering (gasp!) calling another contractor when we made a quick weekend visit to camp. As we pulled in we were met with an astounding sight. There, in the exact spot where we had envisioned a simple stockade fence, was a work of art. In our absence the psychic carpenter had magically appeared and crafted a marvelous structure that looked more like high art than any mere backyard fence. Made of hand finished local lumber, it flowed across the contours of the landscape like a Christo installation and featured a unique basket weave pattern he later told us was "a design the Passamaquoddy tribe used around here a couple of hundred years ago." Indeed. That fence stands today as a silent reminder of a timeless cosmic truth: If you want the job done right, grasshopper, you must trust the psychic carpenter.

Island Stories

While it may be true that "no man is an island," my experience on Maine's islands has convinced me that, over time, each island tends to develop its own quirky and distinct personality. This no doubt stems from the particular challenges inherent in all such isolated communities.

Island life, after all, is inevitably shaped by one common geographic imperative—the fact that people, supplies, energy, and virtually every other necessity must at some point be shipped over from the mainland. There's simply no getting around it. So, while not exactly compelled to become bosom buddies, islanders are highly motivated to develop some degree of cooperation in order to ensure that community life functions smoothly.

That's not to say that everybody gets along, far from it. Anyone familiar with the highly publicized Matinicus Island lobster wars will tell you that when it comes to certain aspects of island life, familiarity can and often does breed shocking levels of contempt. Long before the recent escalation of vandalism and violence among and between the local lobstermen, Matinicus had earned its well-deserved reputation as a tough no-nonsense outpost, populated by independent folks who had their own ideas about interpreting the law of the sea and who gave no quarter to interlopers.

Several years ago I had an opportunity to interview Matinicus's oldest resident. Then nearly ninety years of age, the ironically named Mr. Young, a proud member of one of the island's founding families, had only recently taken to spending his winters off-island.

From October through April he rented an apartment in Rockland. But each spring he headed back down to the docks, loaded his summer provisions into a twenty-two-foot open wooden boat and prepared to make the twenty-plus mile voyage back to his island home.

Just as he was getting ready to cast off, a local fisherman who'd been quietly observing the elderly gentleman's progress with a fair amount of skepticism, asked, "Where you headed?"

"I'm going to Matinicus," replied Mr. Young.

"You got friends out there?"

"Ayuh."

Casting a worried glance toward the open ocean the fellow shook his head and mumbled, "You'd better."

Last summer I was invited to do a performance at the old community hall on picturesque Little Cranberry Island. It was not my first trip to Little Cranberry. In fact I'd been there on numerous occasions, most recently in the late 90s to film a CBS Postcard. On that particular visit I had my first real-world opportunity to practice what Charles Kuralt had once told me was his golden rule of TV journalism.

Shortly after I first went to work for him at CBS News, Charles explained that every now and then I could expect to arrive on location ready to do a story only to discover that the actual story wasn't nearly as interesting as the brass in their offices on West 57th St. back in New York had expected it to be. His advice about how to proceed when faced with such a dilemma? Go out and look for another story.

Our original goal in coming to Little Cranberry that summer had been to interview the postmistress at the tiny island post office. Someone had suggested that she would make a great subject for a story and she'd certainly been animated and enthusiastic in phone conversations prior to our arrival. But when we actually showed up, she acted strangely distracted and even a bit blasé.

The reason for her curious lack of enthusiasm became clear when we learned that her eldest daughter was scheduled to graduate that very evening from the 8th and final grade of the island's tiny K-8 schoolhouse. Naturally enough, the fact that her firstborn would soon be leaving to pursue the remainder of her education off-island occupied her full attention.

We also learned that mom had plenty of reasons to be proud. After all, her daughter had just been elected class valedictorian, not to mention best dressed, worst dressed, class clown, and most likely to succeed. You can add pretty much anything else you like to that list as well since, it turned out, there was exactly one student participating in that year's graduation ceremony and she was that student!

Needless to say, we scrapped the post office story and, true to Kuralt's predictions, the one we ended up broadcasting, called "Island Graduation," was a far better choice. In fact it proved to be one of the most moving and memorable essays broadcast on the show.

The story was all we could have asked for: quirky, funny, and heart-warming. But most of all, it was a story that could *only* have happened on an island in Maine.

Dirt Road Christmas

I was in my mid-twenties, just married, and living in a one-room cabin with a wood stove and an outhouse on a dirt road in Palmyra, Maine. Jimmy Carter was president. Home mortgage rates were hovering around 20% and gas prices had recently doubled. I figured it was the perfect moment to embark upon a full-time career in the arts.

I did okay at first. All summer we got by on what I earned singing "Horse With No Name" in local bars and hand lettering actual names on pulp trucks.

Our nearest neighbors were the Spragues—Forester Sprague, universally known as "Fod," his wife Mary, and their sons, a hardscrabble farm family for whom "gettin' by" was a way of life. About two miles in the other direction was a makeshift commune of young back-to-the-landers from exotic faraway places like Pennsylvania.

As autumn approached, these hipsters packed up their incense, love beads, and wind chimes, climbed into an old school bus, and headed for sunnier climes. Before embarking however, they stopped by to inform us that their erstwhile pet hog Francis Bacon would be spending the winter in the Spragues' chest freezer. If we wanted ham, pork chops, perhaps a pound or two of Francis's actual bacon, we need only drop by and ask. Just ask. No problem, I thought and made a mental note.

Winter came early and hit hard that year. By late November the ground was frozen solid as granite. Finding work was even harder than that.

For the first time in my life I found myself worrying whether we'd have enough food to eat. With Christmas just around the corner, cheer was in short supply.

Then, on a dark December afternoon, it dawned on me. Just a mile up the road there was a freezer full of pork chops, bacon, and maybe even a roast waiting to be transformed into a holiday feast. All I had to do was ask. Is that so difficult? Well, it sure seemed like it to a young man determined to make his own way in the world. Necessity, however, is a great motivator and I soon found myself trudging up the icy road to my neighbors' farm.

Of course, it wouldn't be a short visit. Rural Maine etiquette in a situation like this calls for coffee, a few games of cribbage, and random speculation on topics like the Red Sox and deer hunting. I did just that for an hour and a half, knowing that eventually I'd have to ask "the question." When I finally got my nerve up, Fod's uncharacteristically sharp response startled me.

"You want some of that meat do ya?" he said, fixing me with a withering glare. Then, turning abruptly he called to his wife Mary in the next room and together they clomped noisily down the cellar stairs, returning a few minutes later with several large grocery bags overflowing, not just with the frozen meat I'd asked for, but a month's worth of home grown, home canned beets, corn, tomatoes, relishes and jams, potatoes, and similar staples.

Fod warmed up his truck, we loaded in the groceries, and he drove me home. Even with the heater blasting, the atmosphere inside the cab was chillier than it was outdoors. After we'd unloaded all the bags I turned to say good night. Fod gave me another hard look, crooked his finger in a "come over here" gesture and I walked over and stood face to face with him in the snowy dooryard.

Suddenly, he raised his hand, wagged a finger at me and hissed, "Don't you ever do that again!" I was stunned. Embarrassed doesn't even begin to cover it. Despite the frigid air, I could feel my face burning with shame. "Don't you," he continued, "ever, *ever, ever* sit down the road from me and be hungry again! I simply won't have it!" For a long moment his words seemed to hang in mid air and then they gradually began to sink in.

He continued, explaining that he and Mary had spent countless hours each fall preparing and canning fruits and vegetables and "putting up" various other foods for the coming winter. They'd done this as long as he could remember. As a result, he told me, "We've got good food down cellar we're gonna have to pitch out cause it's been there so long!"

As he said it his whole face exploded into a marvelously warm, wrinkly, gap-toothed grin. Reaching out his hand, he grasped mine, gave it a hearty shake, and said, "Merry Christmas, Tim!" It turned out to be exactly that.

One Final Hug

I was pouring myself a second cup of coffee the other morning when I heard the news. My friend Leon, a local lobsterman and a neighbor back when I was living on Georgetown Island, had been shot and killed in what was referred to as a "domestic dispute." I dropped back into my chair and stared out the window.

The story rambled on, eventually devolving into a repetition of those inane phrases that have become the broadcast equivalent of yellow crime-scene tape: "... police have secured the scene," "... few details are being released," the droning sound track of raw human tragedy. For a split second I felt as though I was the one who'd been shot.

Gradually, details began to emerge. Trust me, I won't re-hash them here. What on earth would be the point? The incident that took my friend's life was simply one more heartbreaking variation on an increasingly familiar theme.

Apparently longing to recapture some vaguely imagined, bygone era, when "real men" settled their "domestic disputes" with six-guns on the streets of Dodge City, America has transformed itself into a nation bristling with firearms of every conceivable size and description. It won't be long before folks start driving Sherman tanks to the local gun show. Maybe they already are.

Is it any wonder then, that the sort of altercation we once rightly expected might result in a black eye or at the very worst a broken nose, is now likely to require the services of a funeral director? I think not, but it's deeply troubling all the same.

To anyone familiar with the ways of Maine lobstermen, a pragmatic, straightforward bunch of folks if ever there was one, it will come as no surprise that my friend Leon lost his life while attempting to help out another person in need, a not entirely uncommon occurrence among this particular demographic. That part of the story at least made some sense to me. Frankly, it's about the only thing that did.

The man I knew, the neighbor I respected and admired for nearly twenty years, was recognized in our little community as a person who expended a lot of his own time, energy, and resources in the service of others less fortunate than himself. He was just like that.

According to Leon, though, he hadn't always embraced such a positive approach to life. In fact, after I'd known him a while I realized that his outward generosity was merely his way of living out a simple inner conviction.

Since others had been there for him when he'd hit rock bottom, Leon figured the very least he could do was return the favor. How do I know all this? That's easy. I was one of those others he helped.

Well over six feet tall, with the kind of working man's heft you don't get from training at the local gym, Leon was the obvious guy to call when I needed help hauling my 26-foot, half waterlogged wooden boat out of the vacant lot across the street from my house, through the center of town, and onto a nearby public boat ramp.

Did I say nearby? I suppose that's always a relative term. Arriving by the dawn's early light in a massive, bashed up 4X4 pickup, its bed randomly splattered with scraps of rancid baitfish, Leon and a couple of his burly friends got right to work. They ended up spending most of one bright sunny Sunday wrestling the bulky vessel through narrow town streets and eventually launching her into the Kennebec.

Of course, since he refused to take any money, I ended up paying him off in Amato's Italian sandwiches, soda, and chips.

It was around this time that I began to suspect Leon's greatest strength had nothing to do with his physical size—quite the opposite. Somehow, my friend with the big heart and the burning desire to help others had acquired strength of a very different sort, the kind that can only be gained via a rigorous course of study at that most unforgiving of all the institutions of higher learning—the School of Hard Knocks.

When I called my wife to relay the sad news, she gasped, then wept. After a long pause she said, "Leon was why Jesus liked to hang out with fishermen."

Then she added, "Getting a hug from Leon was like getting a hug from God." I particularly like that image. I think I'll hang onto it. It's comforting to imagine my friend finally receiving an endless supply of the very thing he so freely gave to all of us.

Yankees Fans Among Us

Two of my wife's younger brothers, both men of the sports minded persuasion, who grew up in Minnesota rooting for the Twins came to visit us a few years back. I'm fairly certain that prior to their arrival in the Pine Tree State, they'd have identified themselves as loyal, enthusiastic followers of the home team.

That particular bit of Midwestern naiveté was promptly dispelled when they arrived back east and had a chance to experience Red Sox Fever up close and personal. As folks around here know all too well, Red Sox Nation in general, and Maine's Red Sox loyalists in particular, are a breed apart—the literal embodiment of a brand of all-out fanaticism for which the term "fan" was originally coined.

"What's with all these people hating the Yankees?" queried my brother-in-law Rich. "Hmmm," I thought. "This is where it starts to get interesting." For Maine's true Red Sox fans, of course, it's not enough to adore the Red Sox. It's just as important to hate the Yankees. Strange as that sounds, it's an article of faith among legions of the Fenway Faithful famous for sporting bumper stickers like, "I root for two teams—The Red Sox and whoever beats the Yankees."

So, is it even possible for a Mainer to be a Yankees fan? Oddly enough I found the answer right in my own backyard. Don't misunderstand me. My mom raised her boys right. We were barely toddlers when she bought my older brother and me cute little matching jackets featuring embroidered baseballs, bats, and gloves interspersed with dozens of Red Sox logos.

Those jackets actually wound up contributing to a non-baseball-related problem for me. Although my brother was a year older, we looked somewhat alike. So, when we wore our spiffy Red Sox jackets, some folks assumed we were twins. Being a year younger, I was a year behind him in school. I'm sure you can see where I'm headed with this. It was an excellent means of acquiring a reputation as "the dumb one."

Am I bitter? Hardly. This is exactly the sort of childhood experience I now realize is absolutely essential for anyone hoping to make a living in the comedy business. If you don't believe me ask Tina Fey or Steve Martin.

So, where were we? Oh yeah, are there really Yankees fans among us? Absolutely. As Exhibit A, I'll submit the following evidence: One of the first sentences I ever heard my Uncle Steve utter was, "I wouldn't go across the street to see the Red Sox play."

He said that right out loud, bold as brass! He may even have added some similar blasphemy along the lines of the Yankees being "okay in my book." I was far too young to fully realize the implications of such brazen apostasy back then. But today, I understand that to make these statements in the presence of impressionable young boys was the Maine equivalent of waving a Russian flag at the McCarthy hearings.

It's also typical of a classic Maine character type, for which Uncle Steve would have made (in many ways *did* make) a great spokesperson. These Mainers are cranky and devastatingly funny by turns. More to the point they're deeply and passionately contrarian. All it takes for one of them to openly embrace a cause is for everybody else to be against it, and vice versa.

As the old Maine saying has it, they're "independent as a hog on ice." You can spot them in a crowd, just keep an eye out for the lone Democrat in an all-Republican town, the atheist at the Pentecostal revival meeting, the Pontiac Aztec owner who'll keep driving hers, thank you very much, until somebody builds a more stunningly beautiful car.

My Uncle Steve went to Heaven many years ago, quite possibly for no better reason than that all his friends were going to Hell. But, I'm pleased to report, Mainers cut from the same bolt of cloth are still among us. A tough, stubborn breed, you'll see them boldly wearing a Yankees cap at the post office during the playoffs and just hoping you'll try and make something of it.

Don't misunderstand me. It's not that these folks actually *hold* views fundamentally different from their mainstream neighbors. In fact it's more than likely that they don't actually give a rodent's hindquarters about the Yankees as a baseball team or franchise or institution or whatever.

What they do care about, and believe me they care about it *passionately*, is driving the true Red Sox fans crazy. Fortunately, given the attitude of the average Red Sox fan, that's apt be a very short trip.

Wear Out, Don't Rust Out

When my great and good friend Helen Carey recently shuffled off this mortal coil, the world lost a marvelous and unique human being. When I say unique, I'm thinking in terms of the dictionary definition: "Unlike any other, the only one of its kind." Well, Helen was all that in a polka dot hat!

Years ago she commuted from her home in suburban Virginia to her real estate office near Capitol Hill in a rather shabby Buick convertible. Shabby? You bet. It had been stolen so often that when the gendarmes retrieved it, as they inevitably did (Sure you'd boost it for a joy ride, but would you really want to keep this beater?), Helen would simply slap another strip of duct tape on the lacerated top and keep driving. Her blasé attitude was no doubt reinforced by the knowledge that she owned a nearly identical model, primrose yellow with leather upholstery, in pristine condition that was available for forays into the suburbs and beyond.

Helen was a true Washington, D.C., insider and over the course of our forty-plus-year friendship she arranged countless cultural expeditions for my benefit. We enjoyed plays at Ford's Theatre, Chinese artifacts at the Smithsonian, The Capitol Steps, the latest Tom Stoppard play, and many more.

Why she never got a traffic ticket on those outings is beyond me. Helen had a tendency to approach the public highway system as if it were her own private go-cart track. She once chauffeured me downtown to some eclectic art exhibit. I can't remember the show, but I'll never forget careening through the D.C. streets in a torrential downpour fervently praying for a parking spot. When Helen's ancient Volvo wagon finally lurched to the curb and came to a shuddering halt in a puddle of rainwater right in front of the museum, I pointed out a sign threatening harsh legal consequences for anyone even *thinking* of parking there. Helen casually dismissed my concerns. "Don't worry," she said airily. "This is my private space. They save it for me." For all I know it was true. The

Volvo was still there, sans parking ticket, when we returned two hours later.

Being that we were fellow anglophiles, it wasn't difficult to talk Helen into sharing a raffle ticket at The Portland Museum of Art one summer afternoon. The grand prize was a week's lodging at a historic cottage in the English countryside. Much to my amazement we actually won!

A grand adventure, eh, wot? Well, sort of, but there would be some logistical hurdles to contend with. Helen was then close to eighty and though her indomitable spirit was undimmed by the passing years, the same could not be said for the aforementioned mortal coil.

Failing eyesight? Check. Poor circulation? Difficulty walking? Check. Check. High blood pressure, narcolepsy? Helen forged ahead completely unfazed, the absolute embodiment of the slogan "Wear out, don't rust out!" She had places to go and people to see. As her traveling companion, however, I felt a certain obligation to make some reasonable accommodations.

With that in mind, I crossed the pond a couple of days early, rented a car in London, reacquainted myself with the joys of driving on "the wrong side of the road," and was standing in the arrivals area at Heathrow when she hove into view.

The Tube ride into Paddington Station was uneventful. The rest of our departure from London, not so much. I'd purchased a large print road map thinking Helen could act as my navigator. Hmmm, it seemed like a good idea until she reached into her bag, extracted a comically oversized magnifying glass, and began scrutinizing the map like Sherlock Holmes looking for clues. I'm almost certain the map was upside down. Three hours later we made it out of London.

As always with Helen, the remainder of the journey—Blenhiem Palace, the Cotswolds, fish and chips in the pub—was similarly colorful and, as always, I wouldn't have wanted it any other way.

I'm not sure what I believe about life after death. Among the more compelling arguments in favor is the incomprehensibility of the notion that such sheer vitality as animates the human form could simply cease to exist.

With that in mind, I like to think that my friend Helen has not in fact vanished into thin air, but rather taken up residence on another plane of existence. There's no way of knowing that of course. But if that *is* the case, I can assure you that wherever Helen has gotten herself off to, the locals are not quite ready for her. That's okay. Nobody here was, either.

One Morning in Maine

Like so many children growing up in Maine and elsewhere in the 1950s, I was introduced to, and quickly fell under the spell of, the timeless works of author and illustrator Robert McCloskey. McCloskey's warm, funny, quirky, yet oddly believable storylines in children's classics like *Make Way for Ducklings* and *Blueberries for Sal* were illuminated by his beautiful and bold original drawings.

Imagine my surprise when Weston Woods, the Connecticut-based production company famous for animated film adaptations of classic children's books like *Mike Mulligan and His Steam Shovel* and Maurice Sendak's *Where the Wild Things Are*, along with several of McCloskey's early works, asked me to audition for the job of narrating McCloskey's last book, *Burt Dow: Deep-Water Man*. It was literally a dream come true. I immediately recorded a sample narration, popped it in U.S. Mail, sat back, and held my breath.

As soon as I got word that I'd passed the audition I gassed up my trusty AMC Hornet station wagon and headed for Connecticut. I already knew what to expect when I arrived at Weston Woods, but the experience was amazing nonetheless. The production studios were located in a series of English style cottages nestled in the beautifully landscaped southern Connecticut re-imagining of an English Cotswold Village. I was shown to my cottage and as I unpacked I noticed the fantastic artwork on the walls. In every room I encountered what appeared to be high quality framed reproductions of great classic children's illustrations. It wasn't until the next morning, while sipping my coffee, that I took a closer look and realized that these were in fact not reproductions at all. They were the original illustrations by the original artists!

I spent the next couple of days working on several slightly different versions of *Burt Dow* and another great children's book, *King of the Cats* by author/illustrator Paul Galdone. I'm pleased to report that both of these productions, upon release, met with both commercial success and critical acclaim. The whole experience was incredible. My only regret was that I hadn't gotten a chance to meet Mr. McCloskey in person. There had been some suggestion that he might come down for the recording sessions but I'd figured that possibility was simply too good to be true and, sure enough, it was. Maybe someday, I thought.

Someday arrived sooner than expected. About a year later I was booked at the Grand Theater in Ellsworth for a Saturday night show in June. The next day being Father's Day, my wife had a surprise planned. I had no idea what to expect as we drove out of Ellsworth early on a bright, clear Sunday morning, made it across the old rickety Deer Isle bridge, parked in a dirt parking lot by a wooden dock, and stood there waiting for something to happen.

Presently a lobster boat approached. I could see that the craft was piloted by a smiling suntanned woman a couple of years older than me. She deftly docked the boat, cut the engine, and hopped out on the dock. Extending her hand, she said "Hi, I'm Sal McCloskey."

I was stunned. Sal McCloskey, as in *Blueberries for Sal*? The very one it turned out. The day that followed was nothing short of magical. Sal ferried us out to Bob's island for a Father's Day luncheon with Bob, his wife Peggy, and Sal's sister Jane. As a lifelong fan of McCloskey's books, I was already intimately familiar with the island and even the cast of characters I encountered that day. That place, the grove of pine trees, the carpet of leafy ferns had all been lovingly and accurately reproduced by the artist in his books, *Time of Wonder* and *One Morning in Maine*.

Bob McCloskey himself could not have been more welcoming. It turned out that he was familiar with my work and had personally requested that I be approached to narrate *Burt Dow*. After lunch he spent some time showing me around his oddly familiar island home. I saw the crescent beach where the osprey wheeled and hovered, the big cleft rock where the children played at low tide, and even the last remains of the blown down tree trunk where the girls searched for treasures after the storm.

My first visit to McCloskey's magical island world marked the beginning of a wonderful friendship. Bob and I hit it off immediately and remained friends for many years, right up until his passing in the summer of 2003. During my time at CBS News *Sunday Morning*, I had the unique opportunity to re-enact that first meeting with Robert McCloskey. Although always somewhat publicity shy, Bob gamely complied as the film crew had him take and re-take scene after scene. The result was one of the most well-loved of all my CBS Postcards and the network received tons of positive responses from viewers around the country. I was obviously pleased and proud. But, nothing will ever top the real life experience of meeting my childhood hero Robert McCloskey and visiting his island home all those years ago on that one very special morning in Maine.

A Strange Symmetry

I experienced an unexpectedly strong emotional response to a Bob Mitchell photo published recently in the *Boothbay Register*. It was a shot of the headstone marking the final resting place of legendary journalist Charles Kuralt.

Nearly two decades have passed since that memorable August afternoon in 1993 when I had my first encounter with Charles. When the phone rang in my office in Bath, Maine, and I was told that Charles Kuralt was on the line, I was naturally skeptical. But his voice was unmistakable and by the time I hung up we'd made plans for a visit the following week.

In deference to the inevitable Maine summer road construction limiting access to my office, I suggested that we meet at the nearby Patten Free Library. I was crossing the rolling lawn, past the lily pond with its William Zorach fountain, when I caught sight of Charles examining the library's recently refurbished gazebo.

We'd barely shaken hands before he began peppering me with questions: "How old is it?" "Is this the original design?" "Who was the architect?" Thus was I introduced to one of Kuralt's signature traits, an unfeigned and boundless natural curiosity that drove him to discover and share countless stories hiding in plain sight along the highways, byways, and back roads of America.

That first meeting led to an audition. Somehow I made the grade and in October 1993, I began what was to become a wonderful eleven-year run as a regular contributor to CBS News *Sunday Morning*.

Now that we were officially colleagues, I soon became acquainted with another of Charles's personality traits. He was incredibly hard to track down—the original "Don't call me, I'll call you," guy. The upside of which was, now and then, he actually *did* call me.

Already a fan of *Sunday Morning*, I knew the show was broadcast live from the studio in New York. So, you can imagine my delight the first time Charles phoned me just as the end credits were rolling with his compliments on that week's Postcard.

Over the next year or so we saw each other infrequently, mostly when I was in the city for production meetings. Unfailingly cordial, but usually running a few minutes late, he was often disheveled and out of breath (chain smoking Pall Malls as he did so enthusiastically will have that effect). Charles was a small man with a large man's magnetism and charm.

A year or so later, Charles retired, passing the *Sunday Morning* baton to the marvelously capable Charles Osgood. He continued to maintain an office at CBS, but good luck catching him behind a desk. He still phoned occasionally, but I was busy and he was busy and the days turned swiftly into years.

I hadn't heard from Charles in several months when I found myself walking across the very same patch of library lawn in Bath, past the same ornate fountain looking more or less in the same direction I'd been looking when I'd first clapped eyes on him nearly four year earlier. Suddenly, I heard a voice say, "I'm so sorry to hear about your friend."

It was July 4th, 1997. I'd been wandering around the annual craft fair on the library lawn when I heard the news. Within minutes I was on the phone with my cameraman Isadore Bleckman. Izzy had spent more than twenty years traveling with Kuralt, filming the *On the Road* TV series. He called from an airport somewhere en route to his home in Chicago and instructed me to meet him two days later at a Doubletree hotel in Chapel Hill, North Carolina. He'd already made our reservations.

So, that's how I came to be in attendance at Charles's interment ceremony in the Old University Cemetery. Standing among friends, family members, and famous colleagues, Izzy and I listened as the U.N.C. president gave a moving and heartfelt eulogy, including a last-minute plot twist absolutely worthy of America's Master Storyteller himself.

Halfway through his remarks, the eulogist produced a handwritten letter, postmarked New York City, July 3rd, 1993, one day before his death, in which Charles requested a burial plot in the very cemetery where we were currently standing. It was a very strange moment, even a little spooky, and I was stuck by the strange symmetry I sensed resonating through this most extraordinary life. As his mortal remains were lowered into the earth, the oddly theatrical arc of Kuralt's own Great American Story became evident, right up to and including the strange dramatic foreshadowing of his own final "sign off," as he left us for the very last time on, you guessed it, the 4th of July.

The King and I

I first met Stephen King in the early 1980s while I was hosting the Annual Cerebral Palsy Telethon on Channel 7 in Bangor. These days the idea of TV telethons is simply a quaint anachronism, like flagpole sitting or marathon dance contests. But, back then these grueling endurance events were the show biz equivalent of the Iron Man Triathlon. True to form, the Bangor UCP Telethon was an all-singing-all-dancing local ham-fest featuring crowds of "entertainers" thrust in front of TV cameras on a cramped, overheated sound stage pretty much around the clock for what certainly seemed to me like the longest weekend in Christendom. Think *Glee* with dozens of not-ready-for-prime-time cast members jacked up on 55-gallon drums of coffee and bushels of high-fructose snack food. Yeeee hawww!

By the time I met him, of course, King was already about as famous as it's possible to get on this planet, so I felt like a horse's aft end when my first words upon meeting him were something like, "Nice to meet you. I've never read any of your books." Smooth move, Timmy.

Amazingly enough, he returned the following night lugging a signed copy of his latest bestseller and, despite our inauspicious start, we really hit it off. Apparently, the psychic bond, formed while acting like complete idiots for hours at a time on live TV, is a powerful one because over the next few years Steve and I developed a great friendship and wound up sharing a number of memorable adventures.

Once, fresh out of one-liners on live TV with about fifteen minutes to fill before the network feed kicked in, we even managed to invent a brand new auction item: "Lunch with Tim Sample and Stephen King at Dysart's Truck Stop." We pitched it feverishly to the highest bidder, "Call now before you think better of the idea!" generating some extra cash for the cause.

Steve King is such an unassuming and genuinely nice man that it's easy to forget that he possesses serious thousand-watt mega-star status. We'd barely taken our seats at Dysart's Truck Stop when we realized our telethon winner had a hidden agenda. Arriving with an unannounced guest, he obviously hoped to parlay his celebrity lunch into a show-biz break for his cousin the magician. Showing up with the young Blackstone wannabe in tow struck me as more than a little presumptuous, but Steve took it in stride and as we quickly learned, the cousin (or brother or nephew, I forget which) was actually an astounding magician.

Everybody knows there's no such thing as real magic. I mean, it's all done with smoke and mirrors, right? I suppose that's true. But, all these years later, I'm still at a loss to find a better explanation for what happened over burgers and fries at Dysart's that afternoon.

The magician introduced himself, produced a deck of playing cards, and prevailed upon Steve to pick one. Admonishing him not to reveal his choice to anybody, the illusionist asked for a pen. I dug out a black felt tipped marker. Steve autographed the card, returned it, and proceeded to re-shuffle the deck and place it face down on the table between us.

The whole thing took maybe ninety seconds and there was simply no way anybody but Steve could have known which card he'd picked. Just about then the waitress brought our meals and we all dug in. During lunch nobody touched that deck of cards. After plates were cleared away we sat back to see what the magician had up his sleeve.

From the inside pocket of his sport jacket he withdrew a plain white envelope passing it around for our inspection. We could all see that it was sealed tight with strips of scotch tape. The magician handed the envelope to Steve and asked him to open it. He did so, revealing the very same autographed eight of clubs he'd drawn from the deck and signed a half hour earlier!

I was stunned! Even the usually unflappable King was impressed. We had no clue as to how the card could have migrated into the sealed envelope while we were all sitting around eating lunch and looking straight at the deck of cards on the table where Steve himself had put it.

Was it magic, metaphysics, a supernatural phenomenon? Who knows? All I can say with any certainty is that the absolute spookiest, weirdest most completely unexplainable event I've ever witnessed just happened to occur while I was seated a few feet across the table from Stephen King. Those are the facts, chummy. I'll let you draw your own conclusions.

VII

Zen and the Art of Storytelling

Good With His Hands

I am not now, nor have I ever been, "good with my hands," handy, or mechanically inclined. Whatever you call it, most Mainers seem to have been born with it. Sadly, the Yankee Ingenuity gene skipped my DNA entirely.

This is, of course, beyond embarrassing in a family where my father once actually built a 36-foot boat in his spare time working nights and weekends. My brothers are the same way. My younger brother can dig a hole, pour a foundation, and build a house right on top of it! I consider this a trick more impressive than David Copperfield's disappearing elephant.

My older brother is the guy with the pickup truck and chainsaw you call after the ice storm. I've watched my youngest sister, a TV producer, command a gauge and dial laden console similar to the one on the bridge of the starship *Enterprise* and single-handedly direct the output of an entire TV station. Me? I'm the guy over in the corner typing with one finger.

As a fledgling dad, I once purchased a "fixer-upper" home. The idea was to save cash while building "sweat equity" by doing a lot of the work myself. Right. Some success with the early "paint and paper" type jobs encouraged me to tackle some of the more structural stuff. I should have quit while I was ahead.

Having decided to build an art studio in the basement, I managed, with the help of some good-with-their-hands friends, to get the Sheetrock installed. Since my involvement was limited to "lugging stuff," this went off without a hitch.

Then I started setting up the studio. The drawing table goes over there. The light table over there. How about a little wooden art stand, something simple and sturdy with a few shelves and maybe some of those swiveling casters on the feet? This is how it starts.

Of course I could have simply purchased something functional for around twenty bucks at Marden's. But we handy homeowners just love our projects, right? I thought, "How hard can it be?" I was about to find out. A couple of hours later and about $512.97 poorer, I headed home.

Not really owning any actual tools of my own, I had felt compelled to purchase some. I'm not sure about the rest of you folk singers, but by the time I unloaded my purchases I certainly "had a hammer," plus two different varieties of power saw (the kind with the big round blade and the other kind with the little skinny blade that goes up and down), a vast selection of screwdrivers, pliers, drop lights, power strips, and about a half bushel of assorted nails, nuts, bolts, and screws. Oh, yeah, and a heavy-duty shop vac for cleaning up afterward, just the basics you understand.

To make my little table sturdy, I'd selected pressure treated 6" X 6" timber for the legs. The top, sides, back, and shelves were made of ¾-inch exterior plywood. Several pounds of galvanized nails, each roughly the size and weight of a railroad spike, and a few dozen strategically placed six-inch woodscrews added strength and durability. The end result was a wooden table about three feet tall by two feet square that took me just over 137 hours to complete and weighed pretty close to 300 pounds. I gave up on the casters because by the time I remembered I had them I couldn't lift the table high enough to install them.

Adding insult to potential major back injury, if you stood in front of my masterpiece with your index fingers on the front corners and pushed gently, the entire structure would wobble around comically like a giant plate of wood grain Jell-O. It was an appalling waste of perfectly good trees.

After sulking for a day or two I called our local carpenter, who came over, looked at my monstrosity, asked a few questions and left. Returning the next morning, he went right to work. Around noon he called me down to inspect his work. In half a day, without breaking a sweat, he'd created a masterpiece of elegant simplicity which, while weighing under twenty pounds, would clearly support a varsity linebacker should the need arise. "No big deal," he said. "I'm pretty good with my hands."

So there it is folks. If you need someone on short notice to keep a couple of hundred people laughing for an hour or so, by all means give me a shout. Looking for help with a few projects around the house? The answer is A.B.T., Anybody But Tim.

Looking for Trouble

I recently spent a few days in the backwoods of Montana visiting my 25-year-old stepson Ben, a seriously outdoorsy young man who grew up hiking, swimming, camping, hunting, and fishing in Maine. I was curious to see how well he'd adapted to life in the Wild West. It only took me a couple of hours in Montana to figure out that, in terms of "outdoorsy," he had landed butter side up. Geographically, Montana is like Maine on steroids. It's several times bigger, with about three quarters as many residents, and, just like here in Maine, there are only a handful of towns and cities scattered among thousands of acres of natural beauty.

Of course, Montana doesn't have the Atlantic Ocean, but it does have the Rocky Mountains, a similar massive geologic presence that tends to elicit feelings of awe, wonder, and humility. Lest you think me a hopeless rube, I should point out that I have been in, over, and through the Rocky Mountains on several previous occasions and been suitably impressed by that whole "purple mountain majesties" thing, while simultaneously managing to block out, minimize, forget, or otherwise avoid the most obvious feature of "them thar hills"—sheer, abject, bone rattling, adrenaline drenched terror. Note to Steve King—even without a homicidal Jack Nicholson prowling around some creepy old resort hotel, the Rockies can be a first rate horror show.

Frankly, I can't believe I'd forgotten that important detail. I really should have known better. In fact my very first family ski vacation in Steamboat Springs, Colorado, left me with a case of nightmare inducing P.T.S.D. Somehow, my wife (who was apparently skiing black diamond trails before she cut her baby teeth) had cajoled me out onto the bunny slope. "This will be fun!" she chirped, while I stood paralyzed on the edge of a seemingly bottomless chasm of ice, rimmed with jagged razor sharp rocks. From that dizzying height, I wasn't able to make out the mutilated remains of the daredevils who'd gone before, but I knew they were down there somewhere. I have no clear recollection of how I made it back to the base lodge that day. The mind has a way of temporarily obscuring that sort of trauma. But it all came rushing back to me as I listened to Ben describing a recent "easy hike" he'd taken with friends.

Apparently the best part of this particular adventure involved standing in the pouring rain on a craggy granite summit just as a massive bolt of lightning exploded a pine tree a stone's throw away. I'd like to think that he was exaggerating the details for dramatic effect, but in fact, I suspect he was actually leaving out the worst part so as not to upset his mother and me. Following the lightning strike a fellow hiker ripped off his shirt and declared, "That makes me feel really alive!" Apparently near death experiences will do that. The next day my wife and I went shopping in Missoula and she bought Ben's new girlfriend an aerosol can of bear repellant as a "getting-to-know-you" gift. "You only have about one and a half seconds to stop a charging grizzly," the cheery salesman said, "so this is much more effective than a handgun." Charming.

The next day we left Ben and headed north toward Montana's world famous Glacier National Park. As we wove our way through the foothills of the Rockies, I had no idea what sheer terror awaited me "up the road a piece." By early afternoon the roads were getting steeper and the scenery more dramatic. At around 3 p.m. I handed a park ranger $25 for the privilege of driving the forty or so miles through the park and crossing the Rocky Mountains via the world famous Road to the Sun through scenic Logan's Pass. If you've ever seen William Blake's illustrations of Dante's Inferno you have some idea of the kind of "scenic" we're talking about here.

By the time I realized what I'd signed up for it was too late to turn back. Stuck in a long line of Subarus and Grand Caravans, I found myself inching up a steep, narrow two-lane road carved out of the side of the mountain range with only the occasional flimsy barrier separating our tiny car from the sheer zillion-foot drop just beyond the passenger door. Just when I thought it couldn't get any worse, big orange "ONE LANE ROAD CONSTRUCTION AHEAD" signs appeared. Obviously, I survived to tell the tale, but the remainder of the drive is an adrenaline soaked blur.

By the time we returned to terra firma I had to peel my cramped fingers off the wheel one at a time before exiting the vehicle in order to prostrate myself in the nearest gas station parking lot and kiss the oily tarmac. It took several hours of 65-mph cruise controlled driving across the table flat farmland of Alberta, Canada, before my heart rate actually returned to normal.

So the next time you're planning an extreme camping trip to the Knife's Edge of Katahdin, or contemplating a bicycle trek to Monhegan, you can count me out. I seem to be able to find enough trouble without actually going out and looking for it.

Answers to Questions
Nobody Was Askin'

I spent most of the morning yesterday drifting around my house like a ghost from a Gordon Lightfoot song, glancing out the window, clipping free ad forms from old *Uncle Henry's Swap or Sell It Guides*, and generally wasting time as I waited for the man from the gas company to drop by and re-light our two auxiliary gas heaters. Have you ever fantasized that *you* have a job where you can say, "I'll be coming to work sometime between 8 a.m. and noon today"? Me, too.

So, why didn't I save myself some cash and the hassle of waiting around and just light the darned things myself? Hmmm, I was kinda hoping we could skip that question. The shocking truth is that I'm not even remotely "handy" in the "home handyman" sense of the term. I recognize the absurdity of a man from Maine making that confession in print. But, there's no way around it. I can barely pound a nail without bending it, and although my wife isn't much better at this sort of thing, we all know that being from away earns her a free pass.

Eventually the serviceman arrived and soon both pilot lights were flickering brightly. Since I was paying for the house call anyway, I asked if he could remove the high tech, digital wall thermostat installed by the previous owners and replace it with something a bit more basic. You know, the kind with an on/off switch and a little temperature adjustment wheel? Something a layman could master without an advanced degree in computer science?

After fiddling with it for awhile he furrowed his brow and muttered, "Any more 'improvements' to these things and pretty soon *nobody* will be able to operate them!"

I've often had that same thought. But somehow hearing it spoken out loud by a full time, honest-to-goodness $65-an-hour professional serviceman felt like genuine vindication. Maybe my kids are wrong to dismiss me as just another Luddite being dragged kicking and screaming into the marvelous new age of technological miracles. Could it be, as I've long suspected, that the world is in fact being inundated by a tsunami of arcane, poorly designed, superfluous gadgets and gizmos all featuring the incredibly frustrating design element of being . . . wait for it . . . answers to questions nobody was asking?

I believe that's exactly what's happening and here's why.

Once upon a time, cars came equipped with large, clear analog gauges designed to provide the driver important information like speed and fuel level at a glance. The idea, quaint as it sounds in today's multi-tasking driving environment, was to enable us drivers to keep our eyes on the road. It was a simple functional system and I don't recall anybody complaining about it, much less wishing that some nameless engineer would invent a digital display too complex and dimly lit to actually read and that disappeared completely in direct sunlight.

Every now and then, when I catch a whiff of ozone, I'm reminded of the original Waring ten-speed kitchen blender. A staple of the American home in a simpler age, it was inexpensive, featured approximately three moving parts, was easy to operate, and capable of reliably slicing, dicing, whipping, and pureeing countless meals and snacks for several generations at a stretch. It was, quite simply, a marvel of form-follows-function design. By comparison, our brand new 127-piece some-assembly-required, high impact plastic food processor with the 300-page instruction book definitely qualifies as an answer to a question nobody was asking.

After paying the serviceman, I drove to the bank to replenish my cash reserves at the ATM—the brilliant technological answer to a question that millions of people actually *were* asking, "How the heck do I get my money when the bank is closed?" I found myself listening to a public radio story about the latest high-tech miracle from Silicon Valley, a driverless car currently under development by Google—that's a relief since we all know computers never develop any serious reliability issues—and already certified for operation in California.

Oh joy! Just what this world really needs, a car you don't even have to drive. Why didn't I think of that? Soon we'll have that thorny problem licked so we can move on to bigger and better things. Why, it's only a matter of time before some genius develops the meal you don't have to eat. How about the thought you don't have to think? Carried to its logical conclusion, I suppose this techno-depravity will eventually culminate in the life you don't have to live—surely the ultimate answer to a question nobody was asking.

Step Back and Squint

Occasionally, when I have no pressing engagements, I like to play a little private mind game. Actually it's more of a mental exercise than a game in that it involves time, popular culture, imagination, historic preconceptions, and perspective, not necessarily in that order. I tend to engage in this sort of mental gymnastics when I find myself sitting in a parked car, staring idly out a window, strolling along the sidewalk, or otherwise occupying the space between life's more immediate, vital, and challenging activities.

Here's how it works: I imagine that I've just mysteriously been plunked down in the current era from some other point in time, usually the recent past, perhaps fifty or sixty years ago. Depending on the circumstances, I might even close my eyes for a moment to enhance the illusion of having made a journey through time. After closing them for a second, I open my eyes and look at the surrounding landscape, attempting to see contemporary life from the fresh perspective of one who has suddenly materialized into now from a half-century earlier.

You might try it sometime. It's surprising how bizarre the most mundane details of twenty-first-century life seem when you step back a few decades and squint. Here then, are a handful of observations compiled from recent voyages in my imaginary time machine:

Okay, it's the future, so I have to ask, what's with all the tattoos? Back when I come from, just about the only tattooed people we ever see are sailors, carneys, and ex convicts. Here in the future apparently everybody, from your kid's kindergarten teacher to the cop on the corner to the latest Oscar nominated Hollywood starlet, seems to have at least a dozen of them prominently displayed.

And was that actually a piece of metal I saw lodged in my waitress's tongue? Ick! Did somebody do that *to* her or is it possible she actually paid someone to have it done? Either way it's too weird to contemplate, especially while I'm trying to decide what to order from the lunch menu.

I have to admit that I'm more than a little bit disappointed about the whole car thing too. After all, this is the future right? Did I miss something? Everybody "back then" knows exactly what cars are going to look like in the future. Frankly, it's one of the few things we all seem to agree on. So, where are the bubble tops, folding wings, and clean, safe, efficient nuclear engines, huh? I've been in the future for several minutes now without spotting a single flying car! I thought they'd at least be zipping around on a monorail while the occupants chatted and sipped martinis. Most of them look like rocket ships anyway, so what's with the wheels? Wheels are so mid-twentieth century. Very disappointing!

And while I'm on the subject, I couldn't help noticing that three quarters of the vehicles these days aren't even cars at all. Giant jeeps? You must be kidding. When did people start driving massive four-wheel-drive trucks with huge metal brush guards to the grocery store for a loaf of bread? Should I be keeping an eye out for stampeding rhinos?

Speaking of keeping an eye out, I've also noticed plenty of those skinny space aliens with the wires sticking out of their heads, blue-green eyeballs and skin-tight stretchy outfits running all over town. What year did their spaceship touch down anyway? Are government agents trying to chase them down? Is that why they're always running somewhere? I've noticed they're not particularly friendly. But, they don't appear to be dangerous, either, unless you consider their level of self-absorption, which probably causes lots of accidents.

Speaking of which, I'm puzzled that despite the fact that cars still have turn signals, almost nobody uses them. Are people telepathic in the future? If so, they apparently still have to move their lips when practicing brain-to-brain communication, as all the drivers seem to be talking non-stop, even when there's nobody else in the car.

Although I always expected time travel to be disorienting, I'm pleased to report that not everything here in the future is new, different, and confusing. One quick glance at the headline in the local newspaper (Thank goodness you haven't gotten rid of the newspapers!) convinced me that politicians have changed hardly at all. Back in my time, they saw communists under every rock. These days they seem convinced that working together to solve our nation's financial problems is "unpatriotic." Still pretty nutty, huh?

Apparently the old saying from my time is still true in yours: "The more things change the more they remain the same."

Where Were You?

It was a Friday afternoon in November and I was a twelve-year-old boy sitting at a desk in the seventh grade classroom of the old Boothbay Harbor Grammar School on School Street. The first afternoon study period was about to begin when a commotion arose out in the hallway.

The flurry of rapid footfalls and raised voices drew a disapproving scowl from our homeroom teacher. Never one to suffer fools gladly, Mrs. Dodge turned abruptly from her chalkboard, crossed the room, opened the door, and stepped into the hall.

When she returned a few moments later her scowl had vanished, replaced by an unsettlingly odd and unfamiliar blank expression. I remember thinking, "Uh-oh, something is terribly wrong."

Later I would come to understand that the look on my teacher's face (and the faces of many other adults in the coming days) was one of pure, unalloyed, mind numbing grief. Closing the door behind her and striding past the now forgotten chalkboard, Mrs. Dodge stopped, turned, faced the class, and, after pausing to catch her breath, proceeded to inform us that the President of the United States had just been shot.

Folks of my parents' generation could, and often did, recount precisely where they were and what they were doing when they heard the news that the U.S. naval base at Pearl Harbor had been attacked. For generations younger than mine, any similarly indelible memory will almost certainly be connected with September 11th, 2001. Yet despite having also experienced the shock of nine-eleven, many, if not most, members of my generation still consider Friday, November 22, 1963, to be the date on which our world changed forever. For us the question is, was, and always will be: "Where were you when you heard that President Kennedy had been shot?"

A half-century later, the events surrounding the assassination of our handsome and charismatic young president, unfolding as they did in real time via fuzzy black and white TV images, seem perhaps even more tragic and incomprehensible than they did back then.

The stark truth is that in those few terrible seconds our nation's destiny was permanently and irrevocably altered, leaving behind a host of painful, haunting, and unanswerable questions: Where would Jack Kennedy's optimism, enthusiasm, intellect, and vision have led the nation? What economic, political, and social changes would have come to pass if JFK had been a two-term president?

Recent research suggests that just prior to the fateful Dallas trip Kennedy seriously considered recalling all U.S. military advisors from Southeast Asia. Had he lived, would we have avoided the Vietnam war? Such missed opportunities are staggering to contemplate. No wonder so many conspiracy theories continue to circulate.

In my view, most if not all of the vast collection of JFK conspiracy theories can be traced to a single, rather poignantly human source—a powerful mental coping mechanism, sort of a neurologic "storytelling software package," by which human beings can create alternate storylines, thus enabling us to make sense out of what is ultimately an incomprehensible and senseless act.

They let us out of school early on that long ago Friday. When I got home, our TV, like just about every other TV in America, was tuned to the unfolding tragedy, almost as if all Americans were trudging hand in hand through some dense fog of national mourning.

Typically reserved Mainers wept openly. Families prepared the usual comfort foods, pies and casseroles. This, after all, is what we do when we've lost a beloved family member. Together, we approached the darkest, most ironic Thanksgiving Day in our memory, a nation transfixed by tragedy. The soap operas were canceled and we awaited the next news update. Yes, the president had been shot. Would he survive? As America prayed, that last flame of hope flickered out shortly after 2:30 p.m., when CBS anchorman Walter Cronkite, choking back tears, confirmed our worst fears.

The now iconic images form a kaleidoscopic panorama of our collective national grief. Jackie's bloodstained dress. The somber funeral procession winding slowly through the streets of the capital and John-John's heart-rending salute as his father's casket rolls past.

Years later, I heard the following oddly moving recollection from a friend and classmate who, as an eleven-year-old girl, was seated directly behind president Kennedy during a Catholic Mass at Our Lady Queen of Peace in Boothbay Harbor in August 1962. She told me she'd spent the entire Mass staring intently at, and virtually memorizing, every detail of the back of this handsome president's head.

Fifteen months later, amid great sadness, that image returned to her, a warm, bright, strangely comforting memory illuminating the darkest of days.

Across the Pond

It's happening again, that old familiar itch that I know from past experience will need scratching sooner rather than later. I can only ignore it for so long before being forced to capitulate. When I can't take it any more I pick up my phone and call Kathleen. Now, don't go jumping to conclusions. It's not what you think.

Kathleen is my travel agent. She's been booking my flights, car rentals, and so forth longer than either of us cares to admit, and, yes, she knows all about my little "itch." Why wouldn't she? She's been helping me scratch it for over thirty years. So, she's never all that surprised when I call sounding slightly panicky and ask (beg is probably a more appropriate word) her to book me on the next flight to London.

Ayuh. The truth is out. This dyed-in-the-wool Mainer is a hopeless Anglophile! And the only thing for it is a trip across the pond. For my "Brit fix" I'll need a few days in dear "Old Blighty."

Like a lot of Americans who came of age in the 60s, the British Invasion of English rock bands changed my life. Seemingly overnight a new crop of hip, cheeky, talented, young Brits seemed to have the world by the tail. And before you could say, "Bob's your uncle," staid, proper old London Towne had transformed itself into Swinging London, the epicenter of an emerging youth, music, and fashion culture that was rapidly transforming the planet

Back then the trendiest threads came from mod shops on Carnaby Street and your new Mini Cooper could be custom ordered with its roof painted like a Union Jack. Sean Connery *was* James Bond on the big screen, while Diana Rigg, playing Emma Peel on the hit Brit TV series *The Avengers*, kept us glued to the small one.

Considering all that, it seems amazing that I somehow managed to postpone my own personal pilgrimage to England until I was a doddering old geezer of twenty-seven.

Naturally, when you've fantasized about a place as long as I had about England, there's always a chance that the actual experience will prove a bit of a letdown. In my case it was just the opposite. From my first glimpse out the airplane window as the sun rose over slate rooftops on the final approach to Heathrow, I was smitten.

On that inaugural visit, I simply walked and gawked and walked some more from one end of London to the other: Piccadilly Circus, Tower Bridge, Hyde Park, Royal Albert Hall, and the rest were everything I'd hoped for and more. For me, London was, and continues to be, a magical place.

Daytrips to the countryside introduced me to the Cotswolds and I paid a visit to Stonehenge when you could still wander around inside the mysterious circle of ancient standing stones.

I recall one particular sun-dappled autumn afternoon spent stretched across the worn leather seat of a train, rocking gently from side to side, past hills and hedgerows, slipping in and out of King Arthur's court via a secret passageway hidden within the pages of my well worn paperback: T.H. White's *The Once and Future King*.

Then an odd thing happened. I found myself thinking, "Now I'm beginning to see why where I live is called 'New' England." Everything, the landscape, the architecture, the climate, even the dialect and dry, understated humor seemed strangely familiar. Those English villages looked a lot like our Maine towns, only several hundred years older. And just hearing their names—Bristol, Newcastle, Bath, and Yarmouth—was like bumping into an old friend.

Shortly after my return, PBS began airing the TV series *All Creatures Great and Small*, based on the popular James Herriot books. Starring some well-known British actors, the shows also featured a few cranky hard-scrabble local farmers from the Yorkshire Dales.

Though I'd never seen any of them before, I recognized them instantly. Their weather-beaten faces, clipped accents, and wry take on life recalled the local characters found at any town meeting, country store, or church supper in Maine.

A year or two later, two British folklorists approached me after a performance and handed me a copy of their recently released album of traditional English dialectical songs and stories, an LP entitled *Ey Up Mi Duck!*

"Ey Up?" I thought. "Now, where have I heard that before?" Then I remembered that old timers around the harbor used to pronounce "Ayuh" almost like that. A longer "E" sound, maybe, like "Eeeyuh," still, just a breath away from "Ey Up"—strange, yet oddly familiar.

No wonder every trip I make to England feels like a homecoming.

A Bump on the Head

When I was a kid, the basic curriculum at our local elementary school included an inspirational tale of scientific synchronicity, in which the young Isaac Newton, innocently snoozing in an apple orchard, is rudely awakened by a lumpy McIntosh caroming off his pate.

The story goes on to suggest that being hit on the noggin' by a falling apple helped kick-start a line of scientific inquiry that eventually led Newton directly to his famous discovery of the law of gravity.

I'm not sure I ever figured out exactly what moral the Newton's Apple story was supposed to convey to a bunch of twentieth-century Maine students (Falling asleep in class will lead to the next big scientific breakthrough?) But, I know why I liked it. In some weird way, I can see how Newton's epiphany may have represented the hope that somehow, my own rather shocking, bump-on-the-head experience might one day yield something of lasting value.

Bump on the head? Oh yeah. It all started innocently enough when, at age ten, I decided to stay after school and play on the playground swings instead of going directly home when school was dismissed. I can dimly recall exiting the school building, hopping onto an empty swing, pushing myself off, and pumping my legs to pick up speed. Yep, I remember that part pretty well. It's the next several weeks that are a complete blank.

Apparently the swing broke apart just at the right moment to send me hurtling skyward, at which point Newton's gravity intervened, returning me abruptly and jarringly to terra firma. The instant my head hit the pavement my consciousness left the premises without even pausing to report the accident.

In audio and film editing there's something called a "butt edit," where you slice into the track, cut out a chunk, then jump in again a bit further down the line. It's also known as a "jump cut," as in, one moment you're here and the next you've "jumped" to someplace over there. That's basically what happened to me in that school yard, only in my case the jump cut didn't happen on film. It happened in real life.

177

One minute I was flying high on the playground swing. The next minute (in regular time that would be several weeks) I was sitting in a hospital room at Maine Medical Center in Portland, listening to a friendly nurse explaining that I would be "going home today."

As she spoke, it gradually dawned on me that, aside from having no idea what or where "home" might be, I hadn't the slightest idea *who* I was! If there's a more startling thought than that I'd like to know what it is.

The feeling of awakening from total amnesia is, of course, impossible to describe. It's something like a 3D version of the sensation you have trying to recall a name that's "right on the tip of your tongue." The information you're looking for is right there, except that it's not. It's hovering just beyond your grasp.

Over the next several days I managed to recall my name, where I lived, and most of the other details of my pre-head-injury life. I say "most" because while virtually everything else came back, those missing weeks simply disappeared. Spooky? You bet.

Oh yeah, there is one more thing. It now appears likely that I emerged from that harrowing experience with something the doctors say I most likely didn't have going in. When my memory returned, along with it came a neurological "glitch" that, back in 1961 when the accident happened, nobody had ever heard of. In exchange for a few weeks of my memory, I'd apparently gained something called non-verbal learning disorder, NLD for short.

Like most kids grappling with undiagnosed, untreated cognitive issues, I took my lumps (both literally and figuratively). But over the years I've come to view my disorder as far more of a gift than a curse. Why? The fact is that a list of classic NLD symptoms includes the following:

Early reader?—check. Excellent grammar?—check. Strong verbal communication skills? Hey, why do you think I've spent most of my life behind a microphone?

Of course not all the NLD news is good. When it comes to math, you can count me out, and the average six-year-old has more refined mechanical skills than I'll ever have.

On the other hand, when it comes to creativity, I'm your guy. In an age when Fortune 500 companies spend millions teaching executives how to think outside the box, I can't even begin to figure out what box they're talking about.

My Stuff

I was surprised the other day when I received an Internet order for a cassette tape of one of my early eighties comedy albums. Though the cassette market has cooled off in recent decades, I believe in planning ahead. So I keep a few on hand for folks like Isaac in Brooklyn, NY, who just shelled out $9.95 for one of these fine collector's items. Having already recouped my production costs during the Reagan administration, I make a decent profit on each sale. Which is part of the problem.

Ah yes, *that* problem. Where to begin? Did I mention that I keep "a few" on hand? Forgive me. I meant to say "a few hundred." At ten bucks a pop, that's still a lot of money, right? Well, sort of. At the current sales rate it will take approximately three and a half centuries to move the remaining inventory. Not exactly a get-rich-quick scheme. And it gets worse.

You know those creepy horror movies where a crowd of zombies dressed in moldy overalls and John Deere caps threatens to overwhelm the village of Pleasantville? Well, something eerily similar seems to be happening to me.

Thankfully, there are no actual zombies involved, but I have found myself besieged by a remarkably similar horde (the operative word here should probably be spelled "hoard") of unwelcome visitors. In my case, the "things" creating all this havoc are just as lifeless, yet weirdly animated, as any member of the living dead ever was.

The way I figure it, a malevolent aggregation of inanimate objects appears to have been following me at a discrete distance for some years now. At this very moment it is garrisoned in my garage, lurking in my laundry room and barricaded in my basement with what I assume to be nefarious intent, quite possibly involving a final assault on my fragile sanity.

Henceforth I shall refer to this mob by its proper scientific name: My Stuff. That's right. It's all mine. There's absolutely nobody else to blame. Step by treacherous step, one innocent little impulse purchase at a time, I alone have singlehandedly created this monster.

Readers of feint heart might want to turn away at this point. But if you think you have the stomach for it, let's take a peek, shall we?

See? Right there, at the bottom of my basement stairs, next to the pile of cassette tapes there are several massive industrial size rolls of bubble wrap. You know, the stuff you use when you're packing up fragile household items?

How long has that been there? Five years? Ten? Who in heck knows? I *do* know that if I ever need to cut up fourteen hundred feet of bubble wrap, one of the 39 pairs of scissors I own will certainly come in handy.

How, you ask, do I know the exact length of my bubble wrap collection? That's easy. I measured it with one of the seventeen retractable metal measuring tapes I have ferreted away in various drawers around the house. See what I mean?

Take that massive, hermetically sealed plastic carton of Legos in the garage (please!). It's been there since our oldest boy left for college. I'll bet there are enough Legos in there to build a structure suitable for human habitation. Darn! I should have donated it to the Occupy Wall Street movement when I had the chance.

Let's see, what else? Oh, yeah, a half dozen table lamps, some mismatched folding chairs, a box of portable cassette players, cameras, and CD players, a nice old boom box with an improvised coat hanger antenna, a perfectly serviceable seat from a 1980 Honda motorcycle . . . (sigh)

It's not as though I haven't *tried* getting rid of this stuff. Yet, somehow, despite yard sales, Goodwill, Salvation Army, the town dump, eBay, and Craigslist, My Stuff is still here.

Unlike the Hollywood version, only time will tell whether this story has a happy ending. But, I'm not going down without a fight. If I haven't looked at it in a year, out it goes! If charities won't take it, the dump certainly will. I don't know if that box of baseball cards contains a Honus Wagner and I don't particularly care. Out it goes! My loss is your gain.

Of course, simply eliminating items already here won't work unless I can also find a way to disrupt enemy supply lines.

Recently I've employed a sophisticated form of Psy-Ops. When tempted to buy something, I gaze intently at the desired object, while imagining it sitting on a yard sale table. I'll keep you posted on the results. But, so far it seems to be working.

It Was Here a Minute Ago

There are few things in life more deeply frustrating than misplacing an item you had in your hand, literally two minutes ago, then spending the next several hours searching for it. I should know. I have a positive genius for this sort of thing.

Whether we're talking about a pair of sunglasses, a cell phone, the car keys, or even a fresh cup of coffee, I have a consistent (and some say downright spooky) propensity for losing things within approximately ten feet of wherever I happen to be standing at the moment.

"Oh," people say. "If that (fill in the blank—pen, wallet, passport, automobile) was really important, you'd have kept a lot better track of it." Nope, in my case anyway, it makes not one whit of difference whether the item in question is a gold Rolex or a bag of potato chips. When it's time to go, poof, it's gone! Heck, one time, many years ago, I managed to misplace a motorcycle for a whole afternoon. Hmmm, now that I think about it, perhaps the less said about that particular afternoon the better.

Let's just say that when it comes to losing things, I'm like Uncle Billy making a deposit at the Bedford Falls Savings and Loan. I stop briefly to chat with Mister Potter. Then I'm standing at the teller's window only to discover all that hard earned cash has evaporated!

Speaking of tellers. At times I swear I must have been channeling Penn and Teller. I'm serious! Real, hard, inanimate, physical objects with genuine heft are there one minute and gone the next. Of course that's absurd. Things never really disappear like that in real life, do they? Even those famous magicians admit that there's no real magic happening. It's just sleight of hand, misdirection, all done with smoke and mirrors. I'm sure that's true. But, it doesn't make it any less baffling when it happens to you.

High on my list of frequently vanished items is my cell phone. Although no great fan of digital technology, I've finally, albeit reluctantly, joined my fellow lemmings. Irritating and dangerous to life and limb as it clearly is, the cell phone is here to stay I guess, although, frankly, in my case, they never seem to "stay" all that long. Perhaps my smart phones have actually become so clever they've figured out how much I dislike them. That would explain why they keep leaving me.

A few years back my wife and I were driving around doing interviews for a book I was writing. Of course we had our cell phones with us. But when we stopped for lunch and I wanted to make a call, my phone had vanished. No problem. My wife simply dialed my number and a few seconds later a ring tone echoed through the car.

A half hour later we still hadn't figured out where the sound was coming from. I was starting to feel as though I was trapped in a *Twilight Zone* episode when my wife pointed out that the ring volume increased each time I leaned forward and decreased when I leaned back. Apparently that'll happen when you sit on a ringing cell phone. Oh well, now I know.

Sadly, not all such mysteries are as easily solved. About fifteen years ago my entire key ring dematerialized in the blink of an eye. This was no sissy key ring either. Heavy enough to generate a decent disability check under the right circumstances, it held several copies of every key to every car, motorcycle, boat, home, garage, camp, office, smelt shack, random padlock, Samsonite luggage set, wall safe, and personal diary anybody in my family had owned for the previous two decades.

Upon discovering the loss, I immediately followed the advice of sci-fi genius Robert Heinlein ("When in danger, when in doubt, run in circles, scream and shout."*), hysterically searching in the same three places approximately 57 times in a row. No dice. For all I knew my keys had slipped through a portal into another universe.

Which brings me to a dream I had as a boy. In the dream I awakened onto a bright celestial plane. An angelic chorus harmonized majestically as I approached a massive white-columned building. Climbing the pristine steps I entered the main hall and noticed a table stretching out as far as the eye could see.

Upon it, carefully laid out in chronological order, I recognized every single item I'd ever lost in my life. Euphoria overtook me. Smiling, I thought, so that's where that went. I knew I'd find it someday!

* from *Time Enough for Love* 1973

Mr. Mellow's Meltdown

Like most folks I've gradually developed an idealized internal image of myself that's often wildly out of sync with the me outside observers experience. That's OK. I understand. They're just wrong. No biggie. See what I mean? I'm an easygoing dude. Call me Mr. Mellow.

I like to think that I'm basically a calm, rational, open-minded fellow. So patient and tolerant I'm surprised the Nobel Prize Committee hasn't called yet. Compared to the real me, of course, this is all a huge pile of Grade-A nonsense, a fact that recently smacked me in the face like a big gooey custard pie.

The other day I fired up my old Mercedes roadster (a mellow ride if ever there was one) and joined the stream of bumper-to-bumper traffic along Route 1. Despite the glacially slow progress my mellow mood never faltered. I simply relaxed, enjoying the warm, sunny weather as, ever the good son, I motored on down to The Harbor to visit my mom.

The first cracks in Mr. Mellow's persona appeared around the middle of the second round of what is currently my mother's favorite game, Upwords—a clever, three dimensional variation on the old classic Scrabble—when it began to dawn on me that I was, once again, being badly trounced by the unfailingly polite, always charming matriarch of Clan Sample.

Taking my intellectual defeat (a more frequent occurrence than I like to admit) in stride , I slapped on a smile and headed back to Route 1 for a meeting with some friends in Yarmouth. Mellow fellow that I am, I even factored in time for the inevitable Wiscasset bridge traffic jam.

Did I say traffic jam? Well, that's certainly what the tourists have to put up with. But not me. Not Mr. Mellow. I just took the local insider's short cut around the backside of Cod Cove and let some polite tourist wave me back into line at the entrance to the bridge. Having thus saved twenty minutes, I was ahead of schedule!

The second slip in my laid back façade came when a fender bender in Brunswick slowed traffic to a crawl, bumping my blood pressure up at least a couple of notches. Grrrrr, this is not good. Mr. Mellow always arrives early. Mr. Mellow is not a time waster. To be perfectly honest, Mr. Mellow is beginning to get just the teensiest bit ticked off.

Once I was on I-295 south of Brunswick, it only took a few minutes of arrogant, inconsiderate, pig-headed driving to get me to the appointed meeting place in Yarmouth. I arrived about ten minutes late. But where were my friends? My phone calls were shunted to voice mail, forcing me to conclude that I'd been stood up. The nerve! Don't they know my time is valuable? At this point, I'd have to say Mr. Mellow had pretty much left the building.

My last remnants of mellowness in tatters, I screeched to a halt in the Maine Mall parking lot and rushed inside to retrieve a pair of glasses my wife had asked me to pick up for her (BTW, my sincerest apologies to the elderly lady I nearly bowled over on my way through the door). Mr. Mellow was now in a full-blown meltdown!

I was returning to my car when my cell phone rang. My friends were wondering why I never showed up for our meeting in Freeport. Freeport? Yup, Freeport, not Yarmouth after all. Oops. The fact that they were having a jolly old time without me just rubbed salt in my wounded ego. But the fun wasn't over yet.

Upon reaching my roadster I attempted to open the trunk only to discover that it was jammed shut and wouldn't unlock even with the key. Yikes! With visions of the jaws-of-life, cutting torches, and thousands of dollars in repair bills dancing in my head I raced over to the Scarborough Mercedes dealership and explained my dilemma. The 12-year-old manager in the service department was extremely patient considering that he was clearly dealing with a hysterical old person.

I explained that the motionless trunk lid was blocking access to my briefcase, which contained my driver's license, photo I.D., credit cards, and, most importantly, my laptop containing my half-finished newspaper column.

As I blathered on, the service manager gently reached down and pressed the trunk release button. The trunk magically popped open. Embarrassed? You bet. Humbled? Plenty.

Reviewing the half-written column, I found myself striking off in a whole new direction, one that I hope you've found interesting. If so, perhaps Mr. Mellow's Meltdown will not have been entirely in vain.

The Lawn Ranger

I've always taken a certain amount of pride in having managed to survive for several decades without doing much of anything that a reasonable person would recognize as exercise. But there's always an exception that proves the rule. In my case, for a guy who swore off workouts sometime in the late 70s as a direct result of an unfortunate experience with a Richard Simmons video, I have maintained a remarkably positive attitude toward mowing my lawn.

Although lawn mowing is at least a moderately vigorous physical activity, it's nevertheless one I've found myself strangely attracted to over the years. The fact that I had some positive experiences with lawn maintenance in my youth may have something to do with that. In fact, one of my first summer jobs involved going door to door asking folks if they'd be willing to pay me a few dollars a week to keep their lawns mowed over the summer. To my amazement several of them actually took me up on the offer and pretty soon my little start-up lawn care business was booming.

I suspect that part of my motivation in deciding to tackle this particular type of work is related to the fact that lawn mowing is an activity generally undertaken only on sunny days. The prospect of being paid to do something, anything, outdoors in Maine, in the summer really got my attention. That the job also involved operating my dad's bright red Toro power mower, a machine uniquely capable of generating that most intoxicating of all summer aromas—the perfect blend of unburned hydrocarbons and freshly mown grass—made it darned near irresistible.

Then again, some of my inspiration may have come from exposure, at a fairly young age, to a small group of adults with a keen interest in grass cultivation techniques. No, not that kind of "grass." Get your mind out of the gutter! I was just a kid for Pete's sake.

I'm talking about the regular old lawn-type grass, a.k.a. turf. You see, around the time I caught the lawn-mowing bug, my dad was a part owner of the Boothbay Region Country Club. Back then the BRCC featured a modest nine-hole golf course, which some local golfers had more-

or-less carved out of an abandoned cow pasture. But even a small course requires a full time grounds crew to take care of seeding, fertilizing, mowing, watering, and generally keeping the greens and fairways appropriately manicured.

After high school I spent several years living in apartments and rental units where there often wasn't even a lawn to cut. Then again, I've owned a few homes with lawns frankly not worth bothering with. Arguably the fanciest home I've ever lived in, located in an upscale Brunswick neighborhood, was sited in a former pine forest where the sandy soil and juniper bushes pretty much foiled any serious attempts at lawn cultivation.

My wife and I finally quit trying, sold the lawn mower, and had our whole front yard roto-tilled. Then we seeded the whole area with about fifty pounds of "meadow-in-a-can." Ironically the resulting riot of colorful summer blooms drew rave reviews from our neighbors.

In sharp contrast, our current home in Portland features a lawn so lush and fertile that we could probably make a living selling turf and, of course, a lawn that grows like kudzu demands constant attention. Returning home yesterday evening and realizing I had barely an hour of mowing time before sundown, I made a beeline for the garage, fired up the mower, and commenced a full frontal assault on my burgeoning hayfield. Generally I'm pretty mellow about mowing. But, this time I was on a mission. The weird weather we've been experiencing in Maine this summer, torrential downpours punctuated by near tropical heat waves, has put the kibosh on my well intentioned plans to maintain a regular lawn care schedule.

Like a man possessed, spurred on by the threat of yet another deluge just around the corner, I carpe-ed the diem, manically power mowing my little corner of suburbia into submission. Exhausted and drenched with perspiration, I parked the mower in the garage and myself in a hot bath. A short while later I was sound asleep.

Awakening the next morning stiff and sore from the unaccustomed exertion, I realized that my days of vigorous lawn mowing may be numbered. Perhaps it's time to consider Plan B, the classic Maine approach to lawn care.

This low-maintenance technique requires a one-time investment in several loads of cement, a few yards of indoor-outdoor carpeting, some strategically placed pink flamingos and a chaise lounge. The result is a year-round, maintenance free lawn and whole lot more leisure time.

My Non-bucket List

Perhaps you're familiar with bucket lists, those classically boomer-centric checklists of things people hope to experience or accomplish before "kicking the bucket." Well, I've decided to compile my own non-bucket list, or maybe I should call it my anti-bucket list.

Whichever title you prefer, here's a short list of things I hope to continue to avoid from now until bucket kicking time.

I hope I never:

1. Own a smart phone
2. Go to the opera
3. Sail around the world
4. Read *War and Peace*
5. Meet Bob Dylan

Let's take it from the top. For me, the tsunami of digital gadgets and gizmos currently flooding our global village represents a lot of answers to questions nobody was asking. I sure wasn't.

Call me a Luddite, but I consider my cell phone an excellent means of remote verbal communication. I take pictures with my camera. I call people on my cell phone. Simple, huh? Although text messaging is apparently the greatest technological breakthrough since the hot tub, I still don't get it. Same goes for tweeting and the next three zillion variations of this nonsense headed our way on the information superhighway.

The notion that every casual thought that crosses our minds is worthy of instant publication throughout the known universe strikes me as being phenomenally self centered, not to mention just plain dumb.

Which, unfortunately, brings us to the opera. I enjoy a wide variety of musical genres, rock, folk, jazz, etc. So what's wrong with opera? I'll tell you what. It's the screaming.

Sue me for boorishness, but I find blood curdling, shatter-the-crystal, full-throated, heart-stopping screaming, even when it's in perfect pitch, to be more than a little alarming. Admit it, if you suddenly blasted fifteen seconds of this stuff at full volume in a crowded shopping mall, people would scatter like chickens, crouch behind the nearest potted palm, and dial 911, or maybe they'd be texting or tweeting. All I know is that I've already heard enough genuine real-life screaming to last a lifetime.

Ah, the dream of sailing around the world sure captures the old imagination, eh? Not mine, chummy! While I find accounts of extreme nautical adventure as morbidly fascinating as the next guy, those fifty-foot waves, man-eating sharks, and the constant threat of starvation can be a real buzz kill.

But, by all means, when you return to dry land after checking "sail around-the-world" off your bucket list, please stop by and tell me all about it. Oh, did I say "when"? Sorry, I meant to say "if."

As an avid reader, I've slogged through my share of daunting tomes, including doorstops like William L. Shirer's *Rise and Fall of the Third Reich* and William James's *Varieties of Religious Experience*. So what's wrong with Tolstoy's blockbuster? I'm not sure. Maybe it's all the hype about it being "the greatest novel ever written." I might reconsider this one, though, but only if Lily Tomlin reads it as an audio book, complete with the funny voices.

Lastly, I sincerely hope to kick the bucket without ever meeting Bob Dylan. Sorry Bob. If I was still twenty years old you'd be at the top of my bucket list. But a lot has changed since then.

Now that I've had a chance to meet people I once admired from afar, including one U.S. president, several bestselling authors, and a smattering of pop stars, I've found that the experience can be oddly disappointing.

I'm not talking about the few celebrity friends I actually know. That's different. I'm talking bout the superficial photo-op, a quick handshake, and then you never see them again except in the photo.

I figure that's the only way I'd ever meet Dylan, in which case I'll take a pass. I mean, what would I say to him anyway? I'd just want to spend hours asking how and why and who and what and, let's face it, if he could explain his music like that he wouldn't have written all those great songs in the first place.

Nope, I'll just keep listening to the CDs and maybe catch him in concert a couple more times.

Meanwhile the rest of you can enjoy following him and everybody else on Twitter, as you sail alone across a vast expanse of ocean, keeping an eye out for shark fins, simultaneously listening to Don Giovanni and wading through *War and Peace* on the latest solar powered, waterproof i-gadget. Oh, and try not to kick the bucket before you make landfall. It'll come in handy for bailing.